DOING HISTO
A Strategic Guide
Document-Based Questions

by Louise Vitellaro Tidd and Charles C. Tidd

Elementary School
Level C–D

aim higher!

Great Source Education Group
A Houghton Mifflin Company
Wilmington, MA

Staff Credits

Editorial
  Robert D. Shepherd
  Stephanie Smith

Layout & Design
  Paige Larkin
  Amanda Sylvester

Consultant
  Harriet Wagnis,
    history teacher, retired, Rockport High School

Acknowledgments

The publisher gratefully acknowledges permissions for use of materials reprinted in this book: Courtesy of the American Foundation for the Blind, Helen Keller Archive, pp. 51–52. (Acknowledgments are continued on page 106.)

Trademarks and trade names are shown in this book strictly for illustrative purposes and are the property of their respective owners. The authors' references herein should not be regarded as affecting their validity.

First Edition

Printed in the United States of America

4 5 6 7 8 9 10   MZ   05 04

International Standard Book Number: 1-58171-471-8

CONTENTS

UNIT 1   PRETEST   1

Lesson 1.1: Understanding Document-Based Questions   11
What Are Document-Based Questions?   11
Taking DBQ Tests   11
Exercise A. Thinking About DBQs   13

UNIT 2   UNDERSTANDING HISTORICAL DOCUMENTS   14

Lesson 2.1: Thinking About Photographs and Illustrations   14
Exercise A. Working with Photographs and Illustrations   17
Exercise B. Question Practice for Photographs and Illustrations   19
Exercise C. Mini-DBQ—Civil Rights March on
              Washington, D.C.   22

Lesson 2.2: Thinking About Advertisements and Posters   25
Exercise A. Working with Advertisements and Posters   28
Exercise B. Question Practice for Advertisements and Posters   30
Exercise C. Mini-DBQ—Westward Travel   33

Lesson 2.3: Thinking About Informational Graphics   36
Exercise A. Working with Informational Graphics   39
Exercise B. Question Practice for Informational Graphics   40
Exercise C. Mini-DBQ—Unemployment During the
              Great Depression   43

Lesson 2.4: Thinking About Letters and Eyewitness Accounts   46
Exercise A. Working with Letters and Eyewitness Accounts   49
Exercise B. Question Practice for Letters and
              Eyewitness Accounts   51
Exercise C. Mini-DBQ—The California Gold Rush   55

Lesson 2.5: Thinking About Newspaper and Magazine Articles   58
Exercise A. Working with Newspaper and Magazine Articles   61
Exercise B. Question Practice for Newspaper and
              Magazine Articles   63
Exercise C. Mini-DBQ—The Great Chicago Fire of 1871   66

Lesson 2.6: Thinking About Official Government Documents   69
   Exercise A. Working with Official Government Documents   73
   Exercise B. Question Practice for Official
      Government Documents   75
   Exercise C. Mini-DBQ—The Thirteenth Amendment and the
      Early Struggle for African-American Civil Rights   78

UNIT 3   WRITING PARAGRAPHS FOR DOCUMENT-BASED QUESTIONS   81

Lesson 3.1: Sentence and Paragraph Writing for the Social Studies   81
   Exercise A. Writing Good Sentences   86
   Exercise B. Making a Rough Outline   88
   Exercise C. Writing a Paragraph   88

Lesson 3.2: Writing Paragraphs for the Social Studies   89
   Exercise A. Analyzing a Paragraph   90
   Exercise B. Outlining a Paragraph   92
   Exercise C. Planning a Paragraph   92
   Exercise D. Writing a Paragraph   93
   Exercise E. Proofreading a Paragraph   94

UNIT 4   POSTTEST   95

ACKNOWLEDGMENTS   106

INDEX   107

PRETEST

This unit contains a Pretest.

You will have an hour and a half to complete the Pretest. Taking the Pretest will teach you what the DBQ section of the New York Social Studies exam is like.

PRETEST: DOCUMENT-BASED QUESTION

Historical Background:

In the late nineteenth and early twentieth centuries, people in the United States started building lots of factories. These factories needed workers. In those days, factories and other businesses often hired children under the age of 16. Some businesses liked hiring child workers because they could pay children less than they paid adults. Many children had to work long hours. Many had accidents on the job or became sick. Often child workers could not go to school and prepare for better futures. By the early 1900s, people began to demand an end to child labor. States started passing child labor laws. In 1938, the U.S. government passed the Fair Labor Standards Act. This law set limits on the ages, hours, wages, and working conditions for young people.

Task:

Write a paragraph that answers this question: How was life different for some children in the early 1900s than it is today, and what was done to change their situation? In your paragraph, use examples from the documents to support your ideas.

Before writing your paragraph, study the documents on the next few pages. Answer the questions about the documents. Answering these questions will help you to write your paragraph.

Part A: Scaffolding Questions

Directions:

Answer the questions that follow the documents. Use information from the documents and your own knowledge. Your answers will help you to write the paragraph in Part B.

LEWIS W. HINE

Child workers in a North Carolina cotton mill, 1908

1. How old do you think the workers in this picture are?

_____

_____

_____

2. What would these children be doing today instead of working?

_____

_____

_____

LEWIS W. HINE

Spinner girl working in a South Carolina cotton mill, 1908. A mill is a factory for processing raw materials. A cotton mill turns the white, fluffy material from the cotton plant into thread, and the thread into clothing.

3. What is this girl doing?

_____

_____

_____

4. Do you think that children should have to do this?

_____

_____

_____

Child Workers in New Jersey, 1903

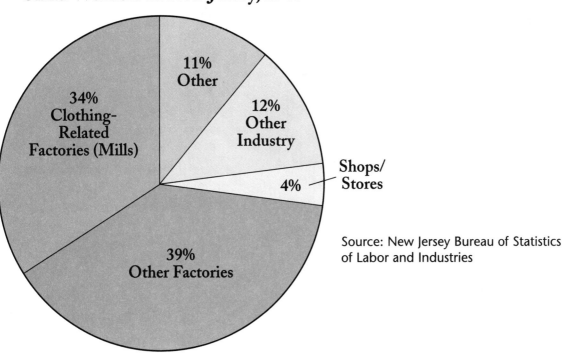

Source: New Jersey Bureau of Statistics of Labor and Industries

5. What percentage of child workers in New Jersey worked in factories in 1903?

_____

_____

_____

_____

In 1938, the U.S. government passed the Fair Labor Standards Act. This poster describes the new rules that the law created.

6. According to the poster, where does a child under 16 belong? Why?

_____

_____

_____

A year ago this magazine considered Georgia one of the most backward states in the Union, from the point of view of the welfare of the children within its borders. We said so, both editorially and in an article written by a citizen of that state. For a time thereafter it seemed to us that half the newspapers of the South were against us, and with them in their criticisms was allied the powerful National Manufacturers' Association. Nevertheless, feeling that the conditions existing, not alone in Georgia, but in many other states, must be remedied, we continued to urge the ratification of the Child-Labor Amendment.... The state knew that its child-labor law was wrong, and to its credit be it said that the old wrongful law no longer exists. As promptly as possible in a matter of such moment, the Legislature went about revising its code for children who labor, and a new law was signed by Governor Walker, August 17th. It went into effect January 1st, and today Georgia has a child-labor law that is as good as any of which we have knowledge.... Georgia may well be proud of its splendid forward step.

Editorial from *Good Housekeeping* magazine, February, 1926. An editorial is a special kind of article in which the writer gives his or her opinion.

7. Is the writer of this editorial for or against changing child labor laws?

_____

_____

_____

8. According to this editorial, why should Georgia be proud?

_____

_____

_____

> *Our very first Christmas at Hull-House, when we as yet knew nothing of child labor, a number of little girls refused the candy which was offered them as part of the Christmas good cheer, saying simply that they "worked in a candy factory and could not bear the sight of it." We discovered that for six weeks they had worked from seven in the morning until nine at night, and they were exhausted.*

—Jane Addams, *Twenty Years at Hull-House*

9. According to Jane Addams's eyewitness account, how many hours did the girls work each day in the candy factory?

_____

_____

_____

10. Why didn't the girls want the candy?

_____

_____

_____

> *...The Secretary of Labor shall provide by regulation or by order that the employment of employees between the ages of fourteen and sixteen years in occupations other than manufacturing and mining shall not be deemed to constitute oppressive child labor if ... employment is confined to periods which will not interfere with their schooling and to conditions which will not interfere with their health and well-being.*

Excerpt from Section 203. Definitions. Fair Labor Standards Act of 1938

11. According to this law passed in 1938, with what should a child's employment not interfere?

_____

_____

_____

_____

_____

Part B: Paragraph Response

Directions:

Use your answers from Part A to write a paragraph. Answer this question: How was life different for some children in the early 1900s than it is today, and what was done to change their situation? In your paragraph, use examples from the documents to support your ideas. Use the lines on this page to begin, and continue on lined paper.

In your paragraph, remember to include

• a topic sentence, or opening sentence, that tells what your paragraph will be about;

• supporting sentences that use examples from the documents to support the idea in your topic sentence;

• a clincher sentence, or ending sentence, that ends your paragraph and finishes your idea.

_____

_____

_____

_____

_____

_____

_____

_____

_____

STOP

LESSON 1.1: UNDERSTANDING DOCUMENT-BASED QUESTIONS

What Are Document-Based Questions?

A **document** is anything written or printed that provides information. Some examples of documents are maps, letters, and photographs. A **document-based question (DBQ)** is one that asks you about written or printed materials. Some document-based questions can be answered in one or two sentences. Others require you to take information from several documents and to write a paragraph or more.

Documents

There are two types of document—primary sources and secondary sources. **Primary sources** are original pieces from a time in the past. Photographs, letters, and newspaper articles are some kinds of primary source. Other kinds include illustrations, posters, maps, and government papers like the Constitution. **Secondary sources** are documents that are not from the time that they describe. Examples include a graph made from historical data or a chapter in a history book.

Types of Question on DBQ Tests

In DBQ tests you will find documents, scaffolding questions, and written response questions. A **scaffolding question** asks about a

particular document. It can be answered in one or two short sentences. The questions on pages 3–9 of this book are examples. Answering these questions helps you to gather information.

A **written response question** requires you to write a paragraph to answer the question. To write a good paragraph, you have to use information from several documents. You begin your paragraph by coming up with a **topic sentence**. This is a single sentence that answers the question in a general way. Then, you use information from the documents to back up, or **support,** your topic sentence. The question on page 10 is an example of a written response question.

Taking DBQ Tests

> Think of yourself as a detective. Study the documents for clues that will tell you about the past. That's what real historians do all the time!

When you take a DBQ test, first read the directions carefully. Read the historical background information. Then ask yourself, "What do I already know about this subject or time period?" You may have already studied the time period and may already know something about it. Next, read the task carefully. This part of the directions tells what your paragraph will be about. Pay particular attention to **key words** that say what you are supposed to do. Here are some key words that often appear in test directions:

Analyze: break something into its parts, describe the parts, and show how the parts are related to one another

Compare: tell about the similarities between two things

Contrast: tell about the differences between two things

Describe: tell about something in detail

Interpret: explain or describe the meaning or significance of something

Support: provide evidence to back up or to prove your main idea

After you have an idea what the general task for your paragraph is, look over the documents. As you look at each document, ask yourself the **reporter's questions:** *who? what? when? where? why?* and *how?*

Who is pictured in the document? **Who** wrote or created it? **Whom** is it about? **Who** was its original audience?

What is the document about? **What** kind of document is it? **What** is the purpose of the document?

When and **where** was the document made?

Why was the document made?

How does the document relate to its time period? **How** did that time differ from today?

Pay attention to any **titles** and **captions** that appear with the documents. A caption is a note placed next to a document to tell you about it. As you study documents, take notes about them on scrap paper. Do not use complete sentences in your notes. Use phrases instead.

After you have studied the documents, answer the scaffolding questions. Use complete sentences in your answers. By answering these questions, you will gather information. You will be able to use that information in your paragraph.

Once you are finished with the scaffolding questions, you can begin work on your paragraph. Reread the written response question and, on your scrap paper, write a one-sentence answer. This will become the **topic sentence,** or main idea, of your paragraph. Next, study the documents and your scaffolding question answers once again to find evidence. Use this evidence in the body of your paragraph to support your topic sentence. (For more information about paragraph writing, see Unit 3, beginning on page 81.)

Exercise A. Thinking About DBQs

1. What is a DBQ?

_____

_____

2. What are some common kinds of document?

_____

_____

3. What is the difference between a primary source and a secondary source?

_____

_____

4. What is a scaffolding question?

_____

_____

5. What kinds of question should you ask yourself when studying documents in a DBQ test?

_____

_____

_____

_____

LESSON 2.1: THINKING ABOUT PHOTOGRAPHS AND ILLUSTRATIONS

Understanding Photographs and Illustrations

Two types of picture that show what life was like in the past are illustrations and photos. An **illustration** is a work of art. Paintings, drawings, engravings, sketches, and cartoons are all kinds of illustration. An illustration is usually printed in a book, magazine, or newspaper.

A **photograph** is a print created from a piece of photographic film. Photography started in the 1800s. Before that time, people used illustrations and other artwork to record people and events.

When looking at photographs and illustrations, take the time to study the details. Ask yourself, "What does this picture tell me about the people and place in it?" Think of yourself as a detective, looking for clues in the picture. Let's see how one student studied the Pretest photo of the child workers in the North Carolina cotton mill.

One Student's Response

LEWIS W. HINE

Child workers in a North Carolina cotton mill, 1908

1. How old do you think the workers in this picture are?

2. What would these children be doing today instead of working?

After Jason read the questions, he knew that he had to look for specific information in the photograph. First, he read the caption, the words near the photo that tell what it is about. The caption told him that the photo was taken in a North Carolina cotton mill and showed child workers. Next, Jason looked for clues. The boys were wearing hats and overalls and pushing wooden carts with metal wheels. Next to the boys was a large machine with spools of thread

---

on it. One of the boys looked like a teenager. The others, however, looked much younger. Jason knew that kids of those ages would today be going to school.

By noticing all these clues, Jason gathered enough information to answer the questions. He wrote, "The workers in the picture include a man, a teenager, and some very young boys. Today, the teenager and the younger boys would be going to school instead of working in a factory."

What to Look for in Photographs and Illustrations

Jason's answer shows how much information can be found in a picture. When studying a picture, think about these parts:

Title and Caption

If a picture has a title or caption, begin by reading it. The title or caption may give you some information about what is going on in the picture and about when it was made.

Subject

Next, study the subject of the picture. The **subject** is what the picture is of, such as a person or an animal. Try to notice everything you can about the subject. What does it look like? If the subject is a person what is he or she wearing? Is the subject happy? By studying how a person or thing looks, you can learn a lot. For example, if the people in a photograph are dressed in fancy clothes, you can make a guess that they are not poor. Such an informed guess, based on facts, is called an **inference.**

Actions

Next, look at what the subject is doing. Is there a specific activity, or **action,** going on, or is the person or subject posing? The boys in the cotton mill photo seem to be pausing from their work to pose for the picture. The little girl is working at a large machine while standing up.

Objects

Objects are the items in a picture that are not the main subject. For example, some objects in the cotton mill photographs are wooden carts, crates, and large thread machines. By studying surrounding objects, you can often learn a lot about the subject. The boys in the cotton mill photo seem to be pushing wooden carts. Their job may have been to move materials of some kind. The little girl seems to be doing a small job on a large machine. Again, such an educated guess is called an inference.

Surroundings

Surroundings are what is around the subject(s) of the picture. Buildings, mountains, a large room—all are examples of surroundings. The boys are surrounded by a large thread machine, windows, and wooden crates, and the girl is standing at a large thread machine. By studying these surroundings you can make inferences about working in the mill.

How to Answer a Question About a Photograph or Illustration

Study a picture and its parts. Then use the information you have gathered to answer the question. You may have to put together several clues from the picture. Suppose that you are looking at the pictures of child workers from the Pretest. You might notice the dirty floors, the wooden crates, the carts, and the large thread machine. Based on

these clues, you can make a guess about the working conditions in the mill. The working conditions for children were probably very simple, basic, and dirty.

When you answer a question, make sure that your response contains only the information requested. Make sure your answer is clear. It should show that you understand how to **analyze**, or study, the document. To do that, state your opinion. Then support it with details from the document.

Remember: Always support your answer with details from the document!

Strategy Review: Photographs and Illustrations

- Figure out what the question is asking.
- Use your own knowledge of history to help you understand the picture.
- Study the title, caption, subject, objects, action, and surroundings.
- Notice details in the picture. Make inferences, or educated guesses, based on these details.
- Answer the question clearly. In your answer, include one or two specific details from the picture.
- Reread your response. Make sure you answered the whole question.

Remember: An **inference** is an informed, educated guess. It is based on details that you have observed. For *all* documents, develop the habit of making inferences about them on your own. The whole secret to understanding historical documents is to study them closely. Notice the details. Then ask yourself, "What conclusions can I draw based on what I have seen?"

Exercise A. Working with Photographs and Illustrations

Directions:

Look carefully at the photograph below. You will answer this question at the end of the exercise: What did this man do to earn his living, and how did he carry the items that he sold?

Man selling water bottles in Mexico City, Mexico, around 1912

1. In your own words, what does the question ask?

_____

_____

Take notes about the photograph.

2. What information does the caption give you?

_____

3. Who is the subject?

_____

_____

4. What is on the subject's back?

_____

_____

5. What do you see in the subject's surroundings?

_____

_____

6. Was this picture taken in the United States? Why or why not?

_____

_____

_____

7. **Answer the question:** What did this man do to earn his living, and how did he carry the items that he sold?

_____

_____

_____

Exercise B. Question Practice for Photographs and Illustrations

Directions:

Answer the questions after each picture. Use what you have learned in the lesson to study the documents.

LINCOLN TAKING THE OATH AT HIS SECOND INAUGURATION, MARCH 4, 1865.—PHOTOGRAPHED BY GARDNER, WASHINGTON.—[SE

March 18, 1865, cover of *Harper's Weekly* magazine. The cover shows Abraham Lincoln's second inaugural ceremony. At an inaugural ceremony, the president takes the oath of office. The new president swears to preserve, protect, and defend the Constitution.

1. What is President Lincoln doing in this illustration?

_____

_____

_____

Bread line following the 1906 San Francisco earthquake. After the earthquake, many people needed help getting food.

2. Why are these people standing in line?

_____

_____

_____

3. What does this photograph tell you about the San Francisco earthquake of 1906?

_____

_____

_____

New York and Cuba Mail Steamship Line. Longshoremen unloading
a ship from Mexico, 1937

4. The men are unloading what product from this ship?

_____

_____

_____

5. Where did the product come from?

_____

_____

Exercise C. Part A: Mini-DBQ—Civil Rights March
on Washington, D.C.

Directions:

Answer the question that follows each document. Then use the information from your answers to write a paragraph for the question in Part B.

The Civil Rights March on Washington, D.C., August 28, 1963

1. What do the marchers in this photograph want?

_____

_____

_____

The Civil Rights March on Washington, D.C., 1963

2. What does this photograph show about the Civil Rights March on Washington, D.C., in 1963?

_____

_____

_____

Exercise C. Part B: Writing About Related Sources

Directions:

Write a paragraph to answer the question below. Be sure to include at least three details from the documents in your answer. Reviewing your answers to the questions in Part A will help you to write your paragraph.

Written response question: How big an event was the Civil Rights March on Washington, D.C., in August, 1963, and what were some of the rights that the marchers wanted?

_____

_____

_____

_____

_____

_____

_____

_____

_____

_____

_____

LESSON 2.2: THINKING ABOUT ADVERTISEMENTS AND POSTERS

Understanding Advertisements and Posters

People often use advertisements and posters to get others to buy or to do something. An **advertisement** is used to sell a product or service. Advertisements appear in many places, from magazines and newspapers to billboards. A **poster** is a large, printed piece of paper that is displayed in public. Some posters are advertisements. They sell products or services. Others provide information or make announcements. For example, you might create a poster to announce a meeting at your school.

Old advertisements and posters can tell us a lot about the past. They show the products, events, and issues that interested people back then. For

One Student's Response

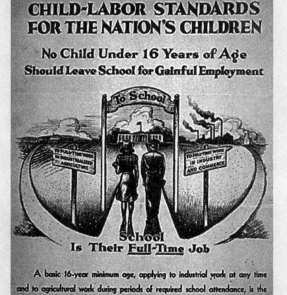

In 1938, the U.S. government passed the Fair Labor Standards Act. This poster describes the new rules that the law created.

6. According to the poster, where does a child under 16 belong? Why?

Lena read the question. She needed to figure out where the creators of this poster believed a child under 16 belonged. First, she read the caption so that she would know what the poster was about. Then she studied the poster very carefully. She looked at the picture on the poster. She noticed a boy and a girl standing under an arch with the words "to school" written on it. The school building was down the path in front of them. She also noticed another heading that said, "School is Their Full-Time Job." She understood that the poster's creators believed that children under 16 belonged in school. Then she knew she had enough information to answer the question. She wrote, "The poster says that children under 16 belong in school and should not be working during school hours. The creators of the poster think that school should be the full-time job of anyone under 16."

instance, the poster on the previous page tells us that people in the 1930s were concerned about child labor. The government, which created the poster, wanted kids to stay in school and not to work at an early age. When looking at advertisements and posters, study the details in them very carefully.

What to Look for in Advertisements and Posters

Begin studying advertisements and posters by thinking about these questions: *who? what? where? when?* and *why?* After looking at the poster or ad, think about *what* you see in it. If it has pictures, what do they show? A picture in an ad may show a product or people using it. The pictures might show what life was like at a certain time.

Next, look at the text in the ad or poster. Advertisements and posters often have several groups of words, called the **copy.** Groups of words might be printed in different sizes. An ad or poster usually has at least one **heading,** or line of text that is very large. The purpose of the heading is to grab the viewer's attention so he or she will read the rest of the poster or ad. The heading may be a **slogan.** A slogan is a phrase that is associated with a product or cause. The rest of the words in the document usually give specific information about the product or event. The heading for the poster in the Pretest is "Child Labor Standards For The Nation's Children." This heading shows the main idea of the poster or what the poster is mainly about. The smaller heading—No Child Under 16

Years of Age Should Leave School for Gainful Employment—shows the opinion of the poster's creators and the message that they are trying to tell the public.

After you have studied what is in a poster or ad, the next step is to think about *whom* it was made for and *why*. In other words, think about the **audience** (whom the piece was made for) and the **purpose** (why the piece was made and what the maker wanted the audience to do). The audience of the poster from the Pretest is the general adult population. The purpose of the poster is to convince people that children under 16 belong in school and should not be working.

Finally, try to learn *where* and *when* a poster was made. If a poster has a title or caption, that may give you some clues. If not, details in the picture might help you figure out the time period. If the picture is a photograph, the poster must be from the nineteenth century or later. Clothing can also give some clues about the time period.

How to Answer a Question About an Advertisement or Poster

A question about an ad or poster may ask about the poster's purpose. It may ask how different parts of the poster, like the image, copy, heading, and slogan, work together. Read the question carefully and follow the steps in the strategies box below. Review the notes you took while studying the ad or poster before you answer the question. Then, write your answer.

Strategy Review: Advertisements and Posters

- Figure out what the question is asking.
- Look at the pictures if there are any.
- Look for headings or large type.
- Read the copy. Watch for slogans and think about what they tell you about the poster.
- Think about the audience, the people for whom the ad or poster was made.
- Ask yourself why the ad or poster was made, or what its purpose was.
- Answer the question.

LESSON 2.2

Exercise A. Working with Advertisements and Posters

Directions:

Look carefully at the poster below. You will answer this question at the end of the exercise: Who was the audience for this poster?

A poster created by the Federal Art Project in 1938 announcing free adult education

1. In your own words, what does the question ask?

_____

_____

Take notes about the poster.

2. What does the picture on this poster represent?

_____

_____

_____

3. When was this poster created, and how do you know?

_____

_____

_____

4. What is the main heading of this poster? What does the main heading mean?

_____

_____

_____

5. What does the information at the bottom of the poster explain how to do?

_____

_____

_____

6. **Answer the question:** Who is the audience for this poster?

_____

_____

_____

LESSON 2.2

Exercise B. Question Practice for Advertisements and Posters

Directions:

Answer the questions after each advertisement or poster. Use what you have learned in this lesson to study the documents.

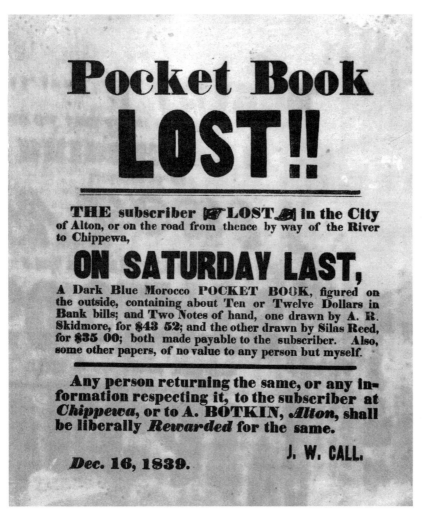

1839 advertisement announcing a lost pocketbook

1. What was inside the lost pocketbook?

_____

_____

2. What will happen if someone returns the pocketbook?

_____

_____

THE
CANADA PATRIOTS.
——————

A Public Meeting of the Citi-
zens of Washington friendly to the cause of Civil and Religious Liberty in Canada, will be held in CARUSI'S SALOON,
this evening, at half-past six o'clock, to express sympathy to-
wards a cruelly oppressed people on our Northern Frontier,
struggling for Independence and Liberal Political Institutions.
Dr. Theller, a Prisoner who re-
cently effected his escape, under circumstances of unex-
ampled peril, from the Castle of Quebec, and Mr. Mackenzie,
from Upper Canada, will attend the Meeting.
Washington, Tuesday, Nov. 20, 1838.

An 1838 poster announcing a public meeting. The purpose of the meeting is to show support for civil and religious freedoms in Canada.

3. Why is this meeting being held?

_____

_____

_____

4. Who will be guests at the meeting?

_____

_____

_____

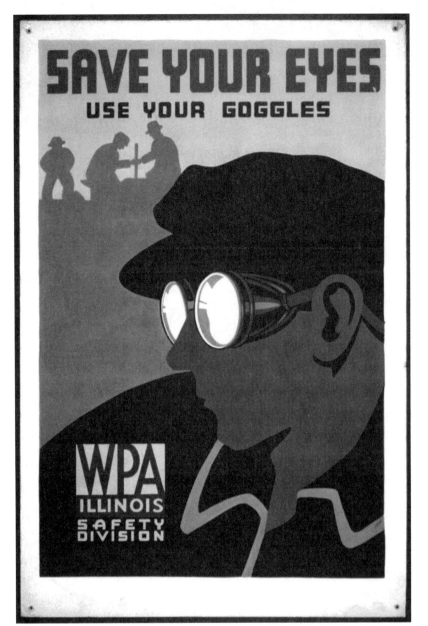

1930s Federal Art Project Poster promoting safety on the job.

5. What is the purpose of this poster?

_____

_____

_____

_____

Exercise C. Part A: Mini-DBQ—Westward Travel

Directions:

Answer the questions that follow each document. Then use the information from your answers to write a paragraph for the question in Part B.

READ FACTS!

During the past fifteen months the present management of the

Missouri Pacific Railroad

Has placed in its track over

7000 Tons of New Steel and Iron Rails

Of the heaviest pattern, thus thoroughly perfecting and renewing the then already excellent condition of the track, and guaranteeing to the traveling public that the trains of *this* Company do not run on

STREAKS OF IRON RUST.

Clearly believing that whatever benefits the passenger benefits the corporation, the Company has supplied the lines under its control with the FINEST LOCOMOTIVES, NEW AND ELEGANT DAY COACHES and PULLMAN'S PALACE SLEEPING COACHES, which are attached to all night trains.

NO DANGER CAN EXIST

Where every modern improvement is in constant use and every precaution taken to carry the passenger *SAFELY* and *SPEEDILY* to his destination.

THE MILLER PLATFORM AND WESTINGHOUSE AIR BRAKE Entirely preclude the possibility of danger attendant upon other roads not supplied with these late improvements.

Speed, Safety and Comfort are guaranteed to purchasers of tickets reading via MISSOURI PACIFIC R. R. For sale throughout the North, East and South, and at Company's Offices, at 115 N. Fourth Street, and Depot, corner Seventh and Poplar streets, St. Louis.

E. A. FORD, Gen'l Pass. Agent, St. Louis, Mo.
GEO. H. HEAFFORD, *Ass't Gen. Pass. Agt., St. Louis.*

Page from a Missouri Pacific Railroad pamphlet, 1860s

1. How has the Missouri Pacific Railroad improved?

_____

_____

2. Read the last section of the poster. What three things does the Missouri Pacific Railroad guarantee to its passengers?

_____

_____

_____

A family poses in front of a covered wagon in Loup Valley, Nebraska, 1886. In the 1800s, many families traveled westward in covered wagons, searching for new homes.

3. What difficulties might this family have experienced traveling in a covered wagon?

_____

_____

_____

4. What are some differences between traveling by train and by covered wagon?

_____

_____

_____

Exercise C. Part B: Writing About Related Sources

Directions:

Write a paragraph to answer the question below. Be sure to include at least three details from the documents in your answer. Reviewing your answers to the questions in Part A will help you to write your paragraph.

Written response question: Why were trains better than covered wagons for traveling westward?

_____

_____

_____

_____

_____

_____

_____

_____

_____

_____

_____

_____

LESSON 2.3: THINKING ABOUT INFORMATIONAL GRAPHICS

Understanding Informational Graphics

A **graphic** is a special kind of illustration that shows facts, or **information.** If you've ever looked in an atlas or made a graph in social studies class, you've worked with an **informational graphic.** There are many different kinds of informational graphic, including maps, bar graphs, pie charts, and timelines.

Informational graphics have many different purposes. For instance, a map might show the location where food is grown in a country. A timeline might show important events in that country's history. A pie chart might show the percentages of the population that live in the different parts of the country. A bar graph might show the number of people who speak different languages in the country. There are many different kinds of informational graphic. This lesson will teach you how to study some of the most common ones. The informational graphic from the Pretest was a pie chart. The pie chart showed where children worked in New Jersey in 1903. Let's see how Roberto answered the question about the pie chart.

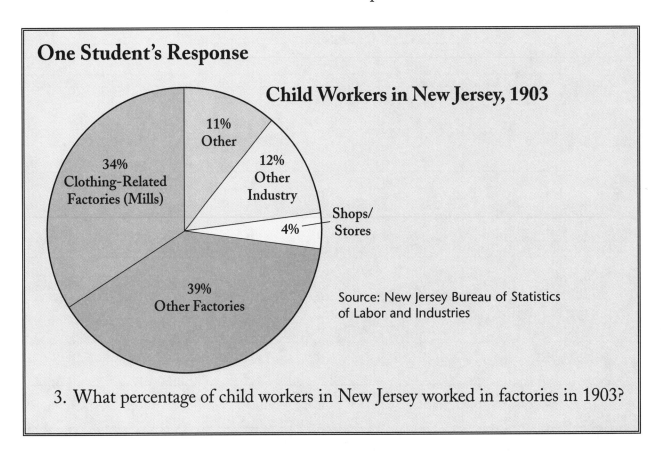

One Student's Response

Child Workers in New Jersey, 1903

11% Other

12% Other Industry

34% Clothing-Related Factories (Mills)

Shops/ Stores

4%

39% Other Factories

Source: New Jersey Bureau of Statistics of Labor and Industries

3. What percentage of child workers in New Jersey worked in factories in 1903?

After reading the question, Roberto knew that he had to find facts from the pie chart. These facts would tell him what percentage of child workers in New Jersey worked in factories in 1903. He looked carefully at the pie chart. He noticed that it had five slices. Each slice was labeled as a different type of job. He also noticed that each slice showed a percentage number. He understood that this number was the percentage of children working in each job category. He looked carefully and saw that 34 percent worked in clothing-related factories and that 39 percent worked in other factories. He added up these numbers and learned that 73 percent worked in factories. Roberto wrote his answer. "Seventy-three percent of the child workers in New Jersey worked in factories in 1903."

What to Look for in Informational Graphics

Title

Look carefully at the title of the informational graphic. The title can tell about its subject or purpose. It might also tell what time period the information is from.

Headings and Labels

Some informational graphics, like bar graphs, also have labels or headings. These give more specific information about the facts in the graphic. Maps sometimes have a **compass rose** that shows directions. A map may have a **legend** or **key** that explains symbols used on it. Most maps also have a **scale** that shows how the distances on the map relate to actual distances.

Details

Some informational graphics contain a lot of information. Try to focus on the most important details. For instance, a **map** might show information about a

specific location, from its mountain ranges to the layout of a town during a certain time. **Timelines** contain information about dates and events. Pay attention to the **sequence** of events, or order in which they happened.

Reading Bar Graphs

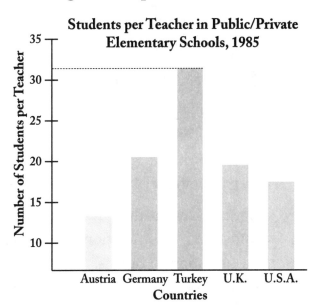

A **bar graph** presents information about two different items known as **variables.** The labels on the graph tell you what the variables are. In the bar graph above, the variables are countries and numbers of students per teacher. You can read the bar graph by starting at the top of one of the bars and running your finger across to the number on the line at the left. The dotted line in the graph shows the path your fingers should trace if you want to find out how many students each teacher in Turkey had in 1985. By following this line, you learn that teachers in Turkey had, on average, more than thirty students in 1985.

What We Threw Away in 1995

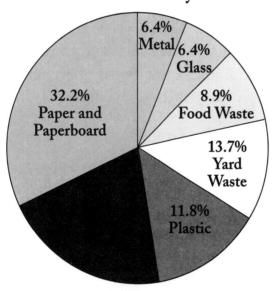

Reading Pie Charts

A **pie chart** is a circle that represents the whole of something. The sections of a pie chart show the parts of the whole. Pay attention to how each "slice" of the "pie" relates to the others. The pie chart to the left shows that in 1995, 32.2 percent of the trash we threw away was paper and paperboard.

How to Answer a Question About an Informational Graphic

When studying informational graphics, make sure to read the title and any labels on the graphic very carefully. For maps, study the legend, or key, if there is one. Notice what items are represented on the map and their relationships to one another. For bar graphs, make sure to ask yourself what the two variables are. For pie charts, pay attention to the parts and their relationships to the whole.

Strategy Review: Informational Graphics

- Figure out what the question is asking you.
- Study the title or caption to see what the graphic is mostly about.
- Pay attention to details.
- Remember to look for values of the variables in bar graphs.
- The scale, compass rose, and legend might give you valuable information about a map.
- Remember to compare the parts to the whole when studying a pie chart.
- Answer the whole question.
- Reread your answer to make sure it is correct.

Exercise A. Working with Informational Graphics

Directions:

Look carefully at the timeline below. You will answer this question at the end of the exercise: What events happened before the Incas built Machu Picchu?

The Expansion of the Incan Empire

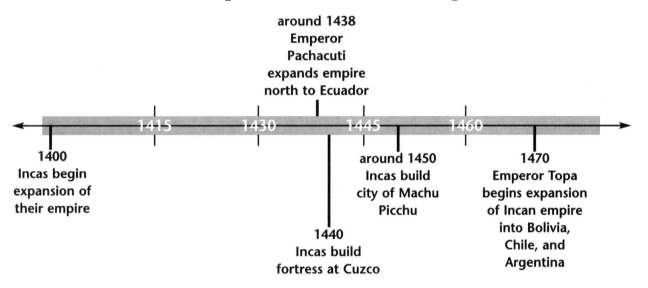

1. In your own words, what does the question ask?

_____

_____

Take notes about the informational graphic.

2. What is the title of the timeline?

_____

3. What is the graphic mostly about? (Hint: Expansion is the process of making something bigger.)

_____

_____

LESSON 2.3

4. List some important details from the timeline.

_____

_____

5. **Answer the question:** What events happened before the Incas built Machu Picchu?

_____

_____

Exercise B. Question Practice for Informational Graphics

Directions:

Answer the question after each informational graphic. Use what you have learned in the lesson to study the documents.

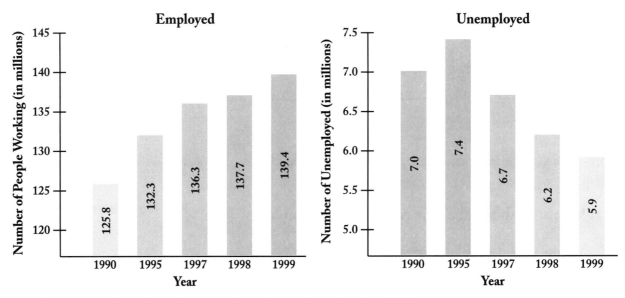

Number of employed and unemployed workers in the 1990s

1. What happened to the number of people working and the number of unemployed workers between 1990 and 1999?

_____

_____

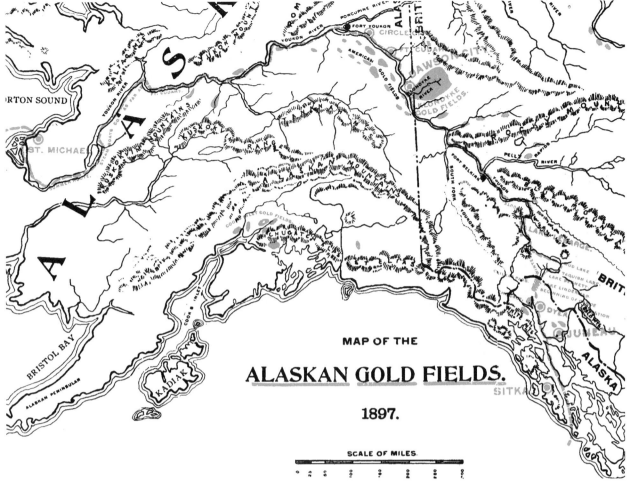

MAP OF THE

ALASKAN GOLD FIELDS.

1897.

SCALE OF MILES.

An 1897 map of gold fields in Alaska and Canada. Gold routes are shown by dotted blue lines. Gold districts are in blue.

2. What is the name of the largest gold field shown on this map, and where is it located?

_____

_____

_____

First Language Spoken by Americans
Born in Foreign Countries, 1910 and 1970

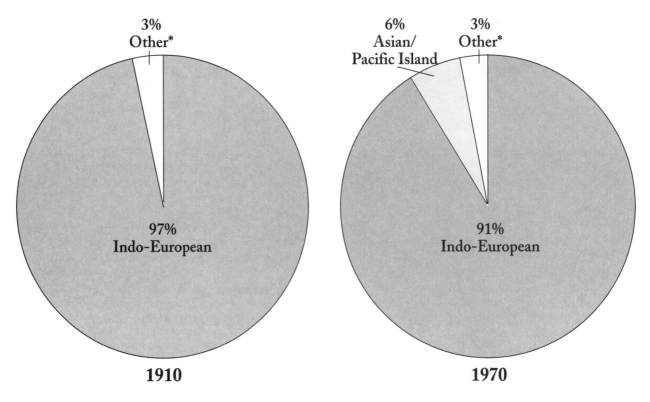

1910 — 3% Other* — 97% Indo-European

1970 — 6% Asian/Pacific Island — 3% Other* — 91% Indo-European

*Other: African, Basque, Caucasian, Native American, Semitic, Uralic
Data collected by the U.S. Census Bureau.

3. What is different about the languages spoken by foreign-born Americans in
   1970 compared to 1910?

_____

_____

_____

Exercise C. Part A: Mini-DBQ—Unemployment During the Great Depression

Directions:

Answer the questions that follow each document. Then use the information from your answers to write a paragraph for the question in Part B.

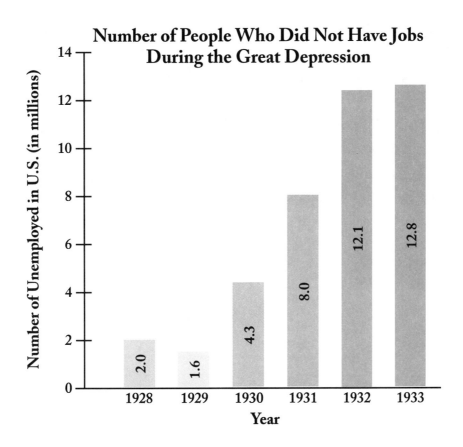

Number of People Who Did Not Have Jobs During the Great Depression

1. What is the subject of this graph?

_____

_____

2. How did the number of people without jobs change between 1928 and 1933?

_____

_____

LESSON 2.3

RUSSELL LEE

Unemployed workers in front of a shack on East 12th street in New York City.

3. What are unemployed workers?

_____

_____

4. What are these men doing?

_____

_____

5. Do the men look happy?

_____

6. Describe the surroundings in this picture.

_____

_____

Exercise C. Part B: Writing About Related Sources

Directions:

Write a paragraph to answer the question below. Be sure to include at least three details from the documents in your answer. Reviewing your answers to the questions in Part A will help you to write your paragraph.

Written response question: How did unemployment in America change between 1928 and 1933, and how did this change affect living conditions for many people?

_____

_____

_____

_____

_____

_____

_____

_____

_____

_____

_____

_____

_____

_____

LESSON 2.4: THINKING ABOUT LETTERS AND EYEWITNESS ACCOUNTS

Understanding Letters and Eyewitness Accounts

When you write a **letter** to a friend, you are writing a private message. Letters are also written for official reasons. For example, people who work in offices often write **business letters.** Sometimes people write letters that they want many people to read, such as **letters to the editor** of a newspaper. Letters are interesting to historians because they can tell a lot about the beliefs, experiences, and feelings of people who lived in the past.

An **eyewitness account** is a document in which someone tells about an event that he or she saw or took part in. Eyewitness accounts can be found in diaries, journals, police reports, court transcripts, and interviews.

When you read letters and eyewitness accounts, it is important to understand the difference between facts and opinions. Both facts and opinions are kinds of statement. A **fact** can be proved to be true. An **opinion** tells someone's point of view. It might tell about a belief, wish, or feeling about something. When you read a statement of fact, you ask yourself, "Is this true?" When you read an opinion, ask, "Do the facts support this opinion?"

Thalia needed to read and understand the eyewitness account written by Jane Addams in her book *Twenty Years at Hull-House.* Here is how Thalia answered the questions.

One Student's Response

Our very first Christmas at Hull-House, when we as yet knew nothing of child labor, a number of little girls refused the candy which was offered them as part of the Christmas good cheer, saying simply that they "worked in a candy factory and could not bear the sight of it." We discovered that for six weeks they had worked from seven in the morning until nine at night, and they were exhausted. —Jane Addams, *Twenty Years at Hull-House*

9. According to Jane Addams's eyewitness account, how many hours did the girls work each day in the candy factory?

10. Why didn't the girls want the candy?

Thalia read the questions carefully. The first asked how long the girls worked each day in the factory. The second asked why they did not want any candy. She read the account and learned that the girls worked in the candy factory from seven in the morning until nine at night. She knew that this meant the girls were working fourteen hours a day. She also read that the girls were exhausted and could not stand the sight of candy. She wrote her answer, "The girls in the candy factory worked fourteen hours a day. They were very tired from their work. They did not want any candy because they were sick of looking at it."

What to Look for in Letters and Eyewitness Accounts

Caption

First read the caption. It might give some information that will help you to understand the piece.

Speaker

The **speaker** is the person who wrote the letter or eyewitness account. Knowing who this person is can tell you a lot. For example, a patriot and a Tory* might say different things about an event during the Revolutionary War. People may understand an event differently because of their beliefs.

Purpose

The **purpose** is why the person is writing. If a speaker is writing to **persuade,** or convince, people of something, think carefully about his or her opinions. Are they based on facts? Do they make sense? Do you share those opinions?

Setting

Ask yourself about when and where the event took place. Recognizing the time and place of the event can help you to make sense of a document.

Main Idea

The **main idea** is what the account is mostly about. The main idea of the eyewitness account from the Pretest is that the little girls were overworked.

Details

Details are the pieces of information in the paragraph that support the main idea. For instance, details that support the main idea in Jane Addams's account are that the girls worked fourteen hours a day in the candy factory, they were sick of looking at candy, and they did not want to eat any.

*A Tory was a colonist who supported the British.

How to Answer a Question About a Letter or Eyewitness Account

When reading a letter or eyewitness account, take notes about it. Think about how the speaker, setting, and main idea work together. For instance, an account of the Civil War Battle of Gettysburg written by someone who fought in it, will be different from an account written by someone who only heard what happened there. After you become familiar with the speaker, setting, and main idea of the letter or eyewitness account, read the scaffolding question. Be sure to answer the whole question, using examples from the document.

Strategy Review: Letters and Eyewitness Accounts

- Figure out what the question is asking you.
- Look for background and setting information in the caption.
- Make sure you understand the main idea or message.
- Think about the purpose of the account and how it affects the message.
- Think about the person giving the account. Ask yourself, "*Who* is writing *what* to *whom*?"
- Read the account carefully and take notes about the details that support the main idea.
- Answer the whole question.

Exercise A. Working with Letters and Eyewitness Accounts

Directions:

Look carefully at the eyewitness account below. You will answer these questions at the end of the exercise: Why is Chief Joseph's heart sick? What are his three suggestions for living in peace?

> *I am tired of talk that comes to nothing. It makes my heart sick when I remember all the good words and all the broken promises. There has been too much talking by men who had no right to talk. Too many misinterpretations have been made; too many misunderstandings have come up between the white men and the Indians. If the white man wants to live in peace with the Indian he can live in peace. There need be no trouble. Treat all men alike. Give them the same laws. Give them all an even chance to live and grow.*

Part of a speech given by Chief Joseph, leader of the Nez Perce Indians, at Lincoln Hall in Washington, D.C., in 1879

1. In your own words, what do the questions ask?

_____

_____

Take notes about the eyewitness account.

2. What type of eyewitness account is this, according to the caption?

_____

_____

3. What is the main idea of this account?

_____

_____

_____

LESSON 2.4

4. List details that support the main idea.

_____

_____

_____

5. What is the setting?

_____

_____

_____

6. **Answer the questions:** Why is Chief Joseph's heart sick? What are his three suggestions for living in peace?

_____

_____

_____

_____

_____

Exercise B. Question Practice for Letters and Eyewitness Accounts

Answer the questions that follow each letter or eyewitness account. Use what you have learned in the lesson to study the documents.

Perkins Institution
and Massachusetts School
for the Blind.

So. Boston, May 3 1893.

My dear Dr. Bell,—
I am truly glad that you were pleased with Helen's "poem." She worked very hard to comply with your wishes; but as it was written in haste she did not have sufficient time to develope her ideas fully and express them as well as she would otherwise have done. I feel that I ought to say this much in justice to Helen.

As I have already telegraphed to you, engagements made sometime ago rendered it impossible for us to leave Boston this week. We will surely start

Letter from Helen Keller's teacher, Annie M. Sullivan, to Dr. Alexander Graham Bell, May 3, 1893

Helen Keller was deaf and blind. Annie Sullivan taught Helen to sign, to read Braille, and to speak. Ms. Keller became a role model for many people. She showed that people who work hard can overcome great challenges.

Dr. Alexander Graham Bell is best known for inventing the telephone. During his life he was also very interested in teaching the deaf to speak. Both his mother and his wife were deaf.

Letter continues on next page →

Lesson 2.4   51

LESSON 2.4

Letter from Helen Keller's teacher, Annie M. Sullivan, to Dr. Alexander Graham Bell (*continued*)

for Washington next Sunday evening.

If it is convenient for you to have us come then we will do so, otherwise we will make different arrangements.

Very sincerely yours,

Annie M. Sullivan.

1. What was the purpose of Annie M. Sullivan's letter to Dr. Alexander Graham Bell?

   _____

   _____

   _____

2. Why was Helen Keller unable to develop the ideas in her poem fully?

   _____

   _____

   _____

TELEGRAM RECEIVED.

FROM 2nd from London # 5747.

"We intend to begin on the first of February unrestricted submarine warfare. We shall endeavor in spite of this to keep the United States of America neutral. In the event of this not succeeding, we make Mexico a proposal of alliance on the following basis: make war together, make peace together, generous financial support and an understanding on our part that Mexico is to reconquer the lost territory in Texas, New Mexico, and Arizona. The settlement in detail is left to you. You will inform the President of the above most secretly as soon as the outbreak of war with the United States of America is certain and add the suggestion that he should, on his own initiative, invite Japan to immediate adherence and at the same time mediate between Japan and ourselves. Please call the President's attention to the fact that the ruthless employment of our submarines now offers the prospect of compelling England in a few months to make peace." Signed, ZIMMERMANN.

The Zimmermann Telegram played a critical role in drawing the U.S. into World War I.

The telegram was sent by German Foreign Minister Arthur Zimmermann to the German Minister to Mexico, Heinrich von Eckhardt. The original telegram was written in code, and the British translated it into English.

The translation was sent to President Woodrow Wilson by Walter Page, U.S. Ambassador to Great Britain, in 1917.

3. What did the Germans intend to do on February 1st?

_____

_____

_____

4. What did Germany promise to give Mexico if it agreed to make war against the United States?

_____

_____

_____

LESSON 2.4

> *Fellow citizens, pardon me, and allow me to ask, why am I called upon to speak here today? What have I or those I represent to do with your national independence? Are the great principles of political freedom and of natural justice, embodied in that Declaration of Independence, extended to us? And am I, therefore, called upon to bring our humble offering to the national altar, and to confess the benefits, and express devout gratitude for the blessings resulting from your independence to us?...*
>
> *Your high independence only reveals the immeasurable distance between us. The blessings in which you this day rejoice are not enjoyed in common. The rich inheritance of justice, liberty, prosperity, and independence bequeathed by your fathers is shared by you, not by me. The sunlight that brought life and healing to you has brought stripes and death to me. This Fourth of July is yours, not mine.*

Speech by Frederick Douglass, one of the best known African-American leaders of the 1800s, to the citizens of Rochester, New York as part of the Fourth of July celebrations, 1852. At that time, many African Americans lived in slavery.

5. Who is Frederick Douglass speaking about when he uses the word "us" in the first paragraph of his speech?

_____

_____

_____

6. Why does Frederick Douglass say that the Fourth of July is not a celebration for all Americans?

_____

_____

_____

Exercise C. Part A: Mini-DBQ—The California Gold Rush

Directions:

Answer the questions that follow each document. Then use the information from your answers to write a paragraph for the question in Part B.

> *We want nothing at this time but a good heavy rain to enable us to wash with more advantage. Had I water, I should make more per day than I do now. As it is I am compelled to use the same water many times in a day till it becomes in muddiness...*
>
> *I live in a tavern... It is called the "Florida House"; board, $12 per week. I sleep in my blankets on the floor, i.e., the bare ground, sound and comfortably for I am used to it. Rise before the sun, roll up and throw my blankets into a corner and, as the sun rises, sit down to breakfast of hot coffee, fresh meat, grizzly bear, venisons, butter cakes, applesauce, etc., etc. then go to work 1/2 mile below the town.*
>
> *Work all day and at night clean up my gold, throw it into a tin box (one we used many years to keep medicine in), put it into one of the capacious pockets of my miner's coat and saunter into town. My pantaloons (over my boots) are at such time covered to the knees with a thick coating of mud and I am splashed from head to foot. But there is no clear water wherewith to wash my face....*

Part of a letter written by Edmund Booth describing his gold-mining experiences in California (1851)

1. Describe what this miner's day is like.

_____

_____

2. What are some of the difficulties he has?

_____

_____

LESSON 2.4

W.H. JACKSON

Three men in a gulch mining for gold (1872). A gulch is a small, narrow, steep-sided valley.

3. Describe the surroundings in this picture.

_____

_____

4. What are the men doing?

_____

_____

5. What tools are the men using?

_____

6. Does the work these men are doing look easy or difficult? Explain.

_____

_____

Exercise C. Part B: Writing About Related Sources

Directions:

Write a paragraph to answer the question below. Be sure to include at least three details from the documents in your answer. Reviewing your answers to the questions in Part A will help you to write your paragraph.

Written response question: What was life like for some miners during the California Gold Rush?

_____

_____

_____

_____

_____

_____

_____

_____

_____

_____

_____

_____

LESSON 2.5: THINKING ABOUT NEWSPAPER AND MAGAZINE ARTICLES

Understanding Newspaper and Magazine Articles

Newspapers and magazines contain **articles** about current events. These articles are written by people known as **journalists**. An eyewitness account only tells one person's view. Journalists try to gather information from several people and other sources for their articles. They try to write about facts that are generally agreed upon and have been proved true.

Articles are usually written to tell people facts about important recent events. For instance, people read the newspaper to find out what's happening in their neighborhood, their country, and the world. Old newspaper and magazine articles can tell us a lot about historical events. They can tell us what facts about an event were known to the writer at the time. Sometimes articles also include people's reactions or opinions.

When you read articles from long ago, you may have some difficulty understanding them. Language changes constantly. You may find that articles written a hundred years ago sound very formal and strange to you today. You might read vocabulary words that you do not know or sentences that are difficult to understand. You might need to reread an article several times to understand its main idea. The **main idea**, of course, is what the article is mostly about.

One Student's Response

Look back at the magazine editorial and at questions 7 and 8 from the Pretest on page 7. Here is how one student answered these questions:

First, Maria realized that she needed to discover if the author of this editorial wanted child labor laws to change or not. She also needed to decide why the state of Georgia should be proud. Maria read the article a few times because she found the language a little difficult. She noticed that at first the author seemed to be against Georgia, calling it a "backward" state. By the end, however, the author was praising Georgia. She understood that Georgia had had some bad child labor laws but that these were changed when new laws were passed in the state. She wrote her answer: "The writer of this editorial is in favor of changing child labor laws in the United States. At first the writer talks about how backward Georgia was and how bad its child labor laws were, but at the end of the article, the writer says that Georgia should be proud because it has passed better child labor laws."

What to Look for in Newspaper and Magazine Articles

Headlines, Titles, Headings, and Captions

A newspaper article almost always begins with a **headline** printed in larger type than the article. There are two purposes to the headline. It should grab the reader's attention. It should also tell what the article is generally about. The **title** of a magazine article serves the same purposes. Often a magazine article will also include subtitles, or **headings,** that appear throughout the article. These tell what parts of the article are about. When a piece, or **excerpt,** of a newspaper or magazine article appears in a book or on a test, it often has a **caption**—a few words that may identify the time, place, author, or subject of the article. Headlines, titles, headings, and captions are useful because they can tell you what a piece is about.

The Five Ws

Reporters have to put a lot of information into their articles. They often try in their writing to answer the questions *who? what? where? when?* and *why? Who* is the subject of the article. It might be a person, thing, or event. *What* is the subject's action, or what the subject is doing. *Where* and *when* are the **setting** of the action—the location and time. *Why* can be the most challenging piece of information to uncover. Sometimes an article will say why something is happening. When it does not, you must combine your knowledge of the other four questions. The setting might help you to figure out why the subject is doing something. You may have to make an **inference,** or educated guess, about why something is happening. Use the facts from the article and what you already know about the time to help you guess.

Main Idea and Details

The **main idea** of an article is what it is mostly about. The specific facts that support the main idea are called **details.** For instance, the main idea of the article in the Pretest is that it is a good thing that the state of Georgia changed its child labor laws. Details supporting this main idea include the facts that the state once had bad child labor laws and that it passed a new set of better laws.

How to Answer a Question About a Newspaper or Magazine Article

Read the question, paying close attention to key words that tell you what to do. Then read the article and take notes on the five Ws as you read. Next, think about the article's main idea. Finally, answer the question, using details from the document in your answer.

Strategy Review: Newspaper and Magazine Articles

- Figure out what the question is asking.
- Scan the article, looking at headlines, titles, headings, and captions that will tell you what the piece is about.
- Read the article carefully. As you read, ask yourself how the article answers the questions *who? what? where? when?* and *why?*
- Think about what the main idea of the article is. Think about how specific facts and other details support this main idea.
- Answer the question completely.

Exercise A. Working with Newspaper and Magazine Articles

Directions:

Look carefully at the magazine article below. You will answer these questions at the end of the exercise: How large is the land described in the article? How much of it was available for settlement and cultivation (growing crops)?

> *Far away in the Northwest, as far beyond St. Paul as St. Paul is beyond Chicago, stands Winnipeg, the capital of Manitoba, and the gateway of a new realm about to jump from its present state of trackless prairies, as yet almost devoid of settlement, to the condition of our most prosperous Western States. Here, bounded on the south by Dakota and Montana, west by the Rocky Mountains, north and east by the great Peace River and the chain of lakes and rivers that stretch from Lake Athabasca to Winnipeg, lies a vast extent of country, estimated to contain 300,000,000 acres, or enough to make eight such States as Iowa or Illinois. Not all of it is fertile, it is true, yet it may be safely said that two-thirds of it are available for settlement and cultivation.*

Part of an article from *Harper's New Monthly* magazine, August, 1882, about huge territory in the Canadian Northwest

1. In your own words, what do the questions ask?

_____

_____

Take notes about the article.

2. In what magazine was the article published?

_____

_____

3. When was it written?

_____

_____

4. Who or what is the article about?

_____

_____

5. What are some details that support the main idea of the article?

_____

_____

6. **Answer the questions:** How large is the land described in the article? How much of it was available for settlement and cultivation (growing crops)?

_____

_____

Exercise B. Question Practice for Newspaper and Magazine Articles

Directions:

Answer the questions that follow each article. Use what you have learned in the lesson to study the documents.

> *The Presidential Election — There was great excitement in the neighborhood of the Newspaper offices and the Telegraph office, last night—a large number of enthusiastic gentlemen having congregated, anxiously awaiting the result of the Presidential election. The first despatch received was that Connecticut had gone for Lincoln by several thousand majority. The next stated that North Carolina was considered certain for Breckinridge. These were soon followed by a brief despatch, which, however, contained the desired information. The Agent of the Associated Press telegraphed that Lincoln's election was certain, and that trifling details were unnecessary. Upon the announcement of this news at the Mercury office, which appeared to be the headquarters for information, the crowd gave expression to their feelings by long and continued cheering for a Southern Confederacy. The greatest excitement prevailed, and the news spread with lightning rapidity over the city.*

Article about the Presidential election results in the November 7, 1860, issue of *The Mercury,* a Charleston, South Carolina newspaper. Charleston is a city in the South. Many people there were against Lincoln. They wanted Lincoln to lose.

1. According to the article, who was certain to win the election?

_____

_____

_____

2. What was the name of the person who ran against Abraham Lincoln?

_____

_____

3. Why were the men in the South Carolina newspaper offices cheering?

_____

_____

_____

4. Were they happy that Lincoln had won?

_____

_____

Clough & Burrell's Fly Trap

We always thought that a lighthouse was intended either to warn the mariner of danger or show some friendly channel; but these inventors call their trap a lighthouse trap, and instead of warning flies of their danger, it, with spider-like guile, allures them to their death.

Our illustration shows one of these traps. The clockwork is in the base, from which rises the central column, which is covered with sand and on which the bait (molasses and sugar) is to be spread with a sponge.

Excerpt from *Scientific American,* September 11, 1858

5. What have Clough and Burrell invented?

_____

_____

6. What does it look like?

_____

_____

EDUCATION

In determining a nation's place and power in the great work of modern civilization, it is not necessary to take into consideration the extent of its territory, the number of its population, the richness of its resources, the extent and prosperity of its commerce, the wealth of its people, the sufficiency of its naval and military defenses, or even the form of its government and the character of its political institutions; the decision must mainly turn on the thoroughness, completeness, and comprehensiveness of its educational machinery and work. Judged by this standard, the United States may fairly claim to be assigned a foremost place in the great community of enlightened and progressive modern peoples.

An article appearing in the March, 1886, issue of *The New England Magazine*

7. According to this article, what are five things that are not as important as education in determining a nation's place and power in the world?

_____

_____

_____

_____

_____

_____

Exercise C. Part A: Mini-DBQ—The Great Chicago Fire of 1871

Directions:

Answer the questions that follow each document. Then use the information from your answers to write a paragraph for the question in Part B.

> *The Chicago fire began on Sunday evening, October 8, 1871, at a quarter before nine o'clock. It raged until half-past ten the next evening, pausing suddenly in a large isolated dwelling-house, which fell into ruins at that time. The work of destruction thus, under the impulse of a driving wind, lasted only about twenty-six hours. The houses destroyed were about fourteen thousand; the people rendered homeless ninety-eight thousand; the value of property destroyed two hundred millions of dollars.*
>
> *The rain of cinders upon the water-works soon made the roof-timbers fall in upon the pumping-engines and block their working-beams. In three or four hours from the outset of the conflagration, the whole city was without water. It lay helpless. Had the wind changed at any time within two days, no part of Chicago would have remained. The historian would have recorded the total erasure of everything above ground. But the wind, which caused the destruction, intervened to limit its extent. It never veered for three days, and thus it held the destroyer to a definite channel widening out to the northwest. The gale blew until it sank down under the smitings of rain.*

Part of an article from *Historic Moments: A Memory of the Chicago Fire,* by David Swing, from the June, 1892, issue of *Scribner's Magazine*

1. According to this story, what caused the fire to spread?

_____

_____

2. How many houses were destroyed? How many people were homeless?

_____

_____

c

c

c

LESSON 2.5

66 Doing History: A Strategic Guide to DBQs

3. Why did the city have so much trouble putting out the fire?

_____

_____

_____

> *The great lesson taught by the last Chicago fire is that measures must be taken not to allow a fire to become... beyond control; a perfect organization of the fire departments on a military basis is essential for this purpose... Another lesson is that it is reckless folly to allow so many wooden inflammable[1] structures to exist in close proximity to one another, and to other buildings, which at the best are only partially fire-proof.*
>
> [1]**inflammable.** easily set on fire

Part of an article from *Manufacturer and Builder,* August, 1874, describing lessons learned from the Great Chicago Fire of 1871

4. According to this article, what two lessons were learned from the Great Chicago Fire of 1871?

_____

_____

_____

Exercise C. Part B: Writing About Related Sources

Directions:

Write a paragraph to answer the question below. Be sure to include at least three details from the documents in your answer. Reviewing your answers to the questions in Part A will help you to write your paragraph.

Written response question: Why did the Chicago Fire of 1871 do so much damage?

_____

_____

_____

_____

_____

_____

_____

_____

_____

_____

_____

LESSON 2.6: THINKING ABOUT OFFICIAL GOVERNMENT DOCUMENTS

Understanding Official Government Documents

Governments create a lot of paperwork. **Official government documents** include all the papers created by or filed with a government. Some government documents, such as speeches given by politicians or records of the actions of Congress, simply tell about government activities. Sometimes, ordinary people have to create or fill out government documents. For example, people complete such documents when they get married, register to vote, or apply for a passport. Historians are interested in government documents because they show a lot about past events. The following chart describes some common government documents.

Act: A decision of a legislative (law-making) body, such as the House of Representatives or the Senate; a law

Bill: A draft of a law to be considered by a legislative body, such as the House of Representatives or the Senate

Birth Certificate: A legal document giving a person's name, date of birth, and place of birth

Constitution: A document presenting the basic law under which a government is formed

Decision: In the law, a document giving a court's verdict in a case, usually including the reasoning behind the verdict

Declaration: A formal statement of what a person or country plans to do, such as a declaration of war

Deed: A legal document showing ownership of a piece of property, such as land or a house

Judgment: In the law, a ruling or verdict made by a court

Legislative Record/Proceedings: A regularly published series of documents describing the activities of a legislative body, such as the House of Representatives or the Senate

Marriage Certificate: A document that has information such as the date and place of a marriage and the names and signatures of the people who were married

Marriage License: A document that gives people the right to get married

Minutes: A record of a meeting

Pardon: A document forgiving an individual who has committed a crime

Proclamation: A statement from a king, queen, or president that has the effect of law

Regulation: A rule given out by a government department or agency and that people have to follow

Speech: An oral presentation to a group of people, such as the Inaugural Address given by the president of the United States

Statute: A law passed by a legislative body

Tax Form: A legal document sent to a local, state, or national government, usually four times or one time each year, showing tax-related information such as wages earned, taxes paid, taxes due, and other such information

Treaty: A document that tells about an official agreement between two or more governments

Will: A legal document made by or for a person to describe what that person wants to have happen after his or her death

The official government document from the Pretest is a part of the Fair Labor Standards Act of 1938. The Fair Labor Standards Act was a law. It told, among other things, how old a person had to be to work. It also limited the number of hours that children could be made to work. On the next page is how one student answered the question about the Fair Labor Standards Act of 1938.

One Student's Response

...The Secretary of Labor shall provide by regulation or by order that the employment of employees between the ages of fourteen and sixteen years in occupations other than manufacturing and mining shall not be deemed to constitute oppressive child labor if... employment is confined to periods which will not interfere with their schooling and to conditions which will not interfere with their health and well-being.

Excerpt from Section 203. Definitions. Fair Labor Standards Act of 1938

11. According to this law passed in 1938, with what should a child's employment not interfere?

From reading the question, Arthur knew that he needed to figure out what a child's job should not interfere with. He read the act over several times because he found the language a little confusing. He learned that a child who was 14 to 16 and was not working in manufacturing or mining could have a job as long as it did not interfere with school or make the child sick. So he wrote his answer, "Children who are 14 to 16 years old can work if their jobs are not in manufacturing or mining, do not interfere with school, and do not make them sick."

What to Look for in Official Government Documents

Type and Purpose

It is important to read the document carefully to learn what type of document it is (a treaty, a bill, etc.) and its **purpose,** or what it is about. As the chart on page 69 tells you, an act is a law. The purpose of the Fair Labor Standards Act was to create a law to set national standards, or guidelines, for both adult and child workers. The law covered pay, overtime, working conditions, and other matters.

Main Idea

A **main idea** is what a document is mostly about. The main idea of the Fair Labor Standards Act is to create a law that sets national standards for adult and child workers.

Supporting Details

Supporting details are pieces of information that support the main idea. Supporting details from the Pretest example might be the fact that a child 14 to 16 can work as long as the job is not in manufacturing or mining and does not interfere with school or make the child ill.

How to Answer a Question About an Official Government Document

Read the question, paying close attention to key words that tell you what to do. Then study the document. Ask yourself what kind of document it is, what its purpose and main idea are, and what details support the main idea. Next, answer the question. Be sure to support your answer with examples from the document.

Strategy Review: Official Government Documents

- Figure out what the question is asking and what kind of document you are working with.
- Read the caption, if there is one.
- Determine the document's purpose and main idea.
- Look for details in the document that support the main idea.
- Think about what you already know about the time the document was written.
- Make sure that you answer the whole question.

Exercise A. Working with Official Government Documents

Directions:

Look carefully at the government document below. You will answer this question at the end of the exercise: To whom did the 15th and 19th Amendments of the U.S. Constitution grant the right to vote and when?

> *Amendment XV*
>
> *Section 1. The right of citizens of the United States to vote shall not be denied or abridged by the United States or by any state on account of race, color, or previous condition of servitude....*
>
> *Amendment XIX*
>
> *Section 1. The right of citizens of the United States to vote shall not be denied or abridged by the United States or by any state on account of sex....*

The 15th Amendment (1870) and the 19th Amendment (1920) to the United States Constitution

1. In your own words, what does the question ask?

_____

_____

_____

Vocabulary: Using Word Parts. Sometimes you can make sense of unfamiliar words by thinking about their parts. Think about the word *servitude* in the selection above. *Servitude* contains the word part *serve*. A person in a condition of servitude is one who is forced to serve others—a slave.

Take notes about the document.

2. What is each amendment's purpose?

_____

_____

3. What is the main idea of Amendment XV?

_____

_____

4. What is the main idea of Amendment XIX?

_____

_____

5. When did these amendments become law, and how do you know?

_____

_____

6. **Answer the question:** To whom did the 15th and 19th Amendments of the U.S. Constitution grant the right to vote and when?

_____

_____

_____

_____

Exercise B. Question Practice for Official Government Documents

Directions:

Answer the question that follows each excerpt from a government document. Use what you have learned in the lesson to study the documents.

> **Washington, D.C., 4th April 1949**
>
> *The Parties to this Treaty reaffirm their faith in the purposes and principles of the <u>Charter of the United Nations</u> and their desire to live in peace with all peoples and all governments.*
>
> *They are determined to safeguard the freedom, common heritage and civilization of their peoples, founded on the principles of democracy, individual liberty and the rule of law.*
>
> *They seek to promote stability and well-being in the North Atlantic area.*
>
> *They are resolved to unite their efforts for collective defense and for the preservation of peace and security.*
>
> *They therefore agree to this North Atlantic Treaty:*

Preamble from the North Atlantic Treaty, April 4, 1949. A preamble introduces a document and tells the purpose of it.

1. According to the Preamble, what were three reasons for establishing the North Atlantic Treaty?

   _____

   _____

   _____

   _____

   _____

Executive Order

It is hereby ordered that from the first Saturday of June to the last Saturday of September, both inclusive, of each year until further notice, four hours, exclusive of time for luncheon, shall constitute a day's work on Saturdays for all clerks and other employes of the Federal Government, wherever employed; and all Executive or other orders in conflict herewith, except the Executive Order of April 4, 1908, relating to certain naval stations, are hereby revoked.

Provided, however, that this Order shall not apply to any bureau or office of the Government, or to any of the clerks or other employes thereof, that may for special public reasons be excepted therefrom by the head of the Department or establishment having supervision or control of such bureau or office, or where the same would be inconsistent with the provisions of existing law.

CALVIN COOLIDGE

THE WHITE HOUSE,
    May 9, 1927.

[No. 4644]

Executive Order by President Calvin Coolidge on May 9, 1927, making Saturday a shorter work day for federal workers

2. According to President Coolidge's Executive Order, how many hours on Saturday will federal employees have to work?

_____

_____

_____

In compliance with Title IV, Section 2, Paragraph 310, of the Revised Statutes of Arizona, I, Alexander O. Brodie, Governor of the Territory of Arizona, do hereby designate and set apart the 5th day of February, A. D. 1904, as

A R B O R   D A Y·

for the Counties of Maricopa, Pima, Pinal, Yuma, Graham, Gila, Santa Cruz and Cochise;

And for the Counties of Apache, Navajo, Coconino, Mohave and Yavapai, I bo hereby designate and set apart the 8th day of April, A. D. 1904, as such

A R B O R   D A Y.

And I recommend that appropriate and instructive services be held in our Territorial institutions of learning and in the public schools, and that a part of the day be devoted to planting trees, shrubs, vines and flowers in public parks and upon the school grounds; and that all teachers and pupils be given the fullest opportunity to participate in the ornamentation of grounds and the perpetuation of the day.

IN WITNESS WHEREOF, I have hereunto set my hand and caused the Great Seal of the Territory to be affixed. Done at the Capitol, in Phoenix, this fourth day of February, A. D. 1904.

Alexander O. Brodie

By the Governor:

Isaac T. Stoddard
Secretary of the Territory of Arizona.

Proclamation of Arbor Day by Arizona Territory Governor Alexander O. Brodie, February 5, 1904

3. What does Governor Brodie want children and teachers from Arizona's public schools to do on Arbor Day?

_____

_____

_____

Exercise C. Part A: Mini-DBQ—The Thirteenth Amendment and the Early Struggle for African-American Civil Rights

Directions:

Answer the question that follows each document. Then use the information from your answers to write a paragraph for the question in Part B.

Amendment XIII

Section 1. Neither slavery nor involuntary servitude,[1] except as a punishment for crime whereof the party shall have been duly convicted, shall exist within the United States, or any place subject to their jurisdiction.[2]

Section 2. Congress shall have power to enforce this article by appropriate legislation.[3]

[1]**involuntary servitude.** work done for another person against one's will

[2]**jurisdiction.** an area under the control of a government

[3]**legislation.** laws

The 13th Amendment (1865) to the United States Constitution

1. What effect did the Thirteenth Amendment have on slavery in the United States?

_____

_____

_____

_____

_____

_____

Besides the right to testify and the right to vote, there are other rights without which Equality does not exist....

The new made citizen is called to travel for business, for health, or for pleasure; but here his trials begin. His money, whether gold or paper, is the same as the white man's; but the doors of the public hotel...close against him, and the public conveyances [such as railroads] which the...law declares equally free to all alike, have no such freedom for him. He longs, perhaps, for [rest] and relaxation at some place of public amusement...and here also the same...discrimination is made....Seeking the welfare of his child, he strives to [give him an] education, and takes him affectionately to the common school...but these doors slam rudely in the face of the child....And the same [insult] shows itself in other institutions of science and learning, also in the church and in the last resting place on earth.

Part of a speech given in 1872 by Senator Charles Sumner of Massachusetts. He was arguing for stronger laws to protect civil rights.

2. After the Civil War, an amendment to the Constitution outlawed slavery and made the newly free African Americans into citizens of the United States. According to Senator Sumner, what problems did these new citizens face in the late 1800s?

_____

_____

_____

_____

_____

Directions:

Write a paragraph to answer the question below. Be sure to include at least three details from the documents in your answer. Reviewing your answers to the questions in Part A will help you to write your paragraph.

Written response question: What effect did the Thirteenth Amendment have on the lives of African Americans in the United States, and why were more laws needed to protect the rights of African Americans?

_____

_____

_____

_____

_____

_____

_____

_____

_____

_____

_____

LESSON 3.1: SENTENCE AND PARAGRAPH WRITING FOR THE SOCIAL STUDIES

As you have seen, DBQ tests usually contain two kinds of question: scaffolding questions and written-response questions. **Scaffolding questions** can usually be answered in one or two sentences. Occasionally, you might want to write three or four sentences to answer a scaffolding question completely. **Written-response questions** require a longer answer. In this lesson you will learn how to write good sentences and the paragraphs that make up a DBQ written response. In Lesson 3.2, you will learn how to analyze a paragraph response.

Writing Sentences

A **sentence** is a group of words that expresses a single complete idea. A sentence must contain at least one **subject** (what the sentence is about) and one **verb** (an action word that tells what the subject is doing, or a state-of-being word such as *am, are, is, was, were,* or *be*).

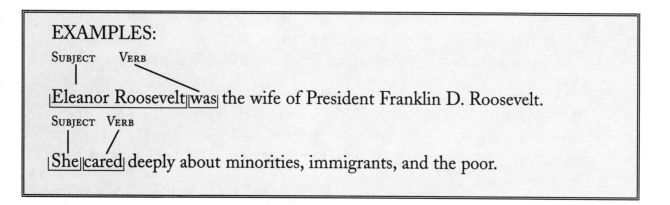

EXAMPLES:

SUBJECT VERB

|Eleanor Roosevelt||was| the wife of President Franklin D. Roosevelt.

SUBJECT VERB

|She||cared| deeply about minorities, immigrants, and the poor.

The following chart explains some important rules to keep in mind when writing sentences:

Guidelines for Writing Sentences

1. Make sure that every sentence contains a subject and a verb.
2. Make sure that every sentence begins with a capital letter.
3. Make sure that every sentence ends with an end mark—a period (.), a question mark (?), or an exclamation mark (!).
4. Keep your sentences interesting by starting them in different ways and by writing sentences of different lengths. *continues on next page*

DULL: Eleanor Roosevelt was President Franklin D. Roosevelt's wife. She wanted to help minorities and women. She learned about their plight. She was interested in civil rights. She traveled all over the United States. She became the "eyes and ears" of her husband.

MORE INTERESTING: Eleanor Roosevelt, the wife of President Franklin D. Roosevelt, dedicated herself to helping minorities and women gain civil rights. She traveled all over the country in order to understand the state of race relations and women's situations and became the "eyes and ears" of her husband.

5. Writing in the social studies contains lots of **proper nouns**—names of people, places, and events. It also contains **proper adjectives**—descriptive words made from proper nouns. Make sure that you capitalize proper nouns and adjectives when writing your sentences.

   INCORRECT: When america entered world war II, eleanor roosevelt continued to fight for civil rights for minorities. She did not understand how americans could justify fighting against racism on european soil while tolerating it here at home.

   CORRECT: When America entered World War II, Eleanor Roosevelt continued to fight for civil rights for minorities. She did not understand how Americans could justify fighting against racism on European soil while tolerating it here at home.

6. Avoid sentence fragments—groups of words that do not contain a subject and a verb or that do not express a complete idea.

   FRAGMENT: worked tirelessly for equal rights for women. (The group of words is missing a subject.)

   COMPLETE SENTENCE: Eleanor Roosevelt worked tirelessly for equal rights for women.

7. Avoid run-on sentences—ones in which two sentences are run together without an end mark to separate them.

   RUN-ON: Eleanor Roosevelt was a strong woman she did not let criticism slow her down.

   CORRECTED: Eleanor Roosevelt was a strong woman. She did not let criticism slow her down.

8. Use quotation marks around words quoted directly from a source.

   EXAMPLE: Eleanor Roosevelt once said, "You get more joy out of the giving to others, and should put a good deal of thought into the happiness you are able to give."

Writing Paragraphs

When you write a response for a DBQ exam, you should answer the question using proper paragraph form.

What Is a Paragraph?

A **paragraph** is a group of sentences about a single main idea. Read the following example:

Topic sentence

President John F. Kennedy visited West Germany on a trip in June of 1963 in order to show America's continuing support for its allies and to spread good will.

Body sentences

One of the places that he visited was the city of Berlin. Like Germany itself, the city of Berlin had been divided into two spheres of influence after the defeat of the Nazis in World War II. East and West Germany soon became the focus of political tension during the Cold War era. For example, in 1948, the Soviets placed a blockade on West Berlin's railroads, highways, and waterways. Consequently, the U.S. and Great Britain spent eleven months airlifting in vital supplies the city needed to survive in defiance of the blockade. In 1961, the East Germans began building the Berlin Wall, which would eventually encircle the perimeter of West Berlin. The wall was erected to prevent anyone from crossing over into the West and gaining freedom. It was during the 1963 visit that President Kennedy told West Berliners, "Ich bin ein Berliner" (I am a Berliner). These words were enthusiastically received by the citizens of West Berlin.

Clincher sentence

President Kennedy's visit was an important event for the city and its inhabitants because it reinforced America's commitment to support freedom and democracy in West Germany.

A well-written paragraph contains several parts, as follows:

Parts of a Paragraph

- The **topic sentence** gives the main idea of the paragraph.
- The **body sentences** provide details that support the main idea of the paragraph.
- The **clincher sentence** sums up the paragraph.

In the paragraph about President Kennedy, the first sentence is the topic sentence. It tells you that the paragraph will be about President Kennedy's trip to West Germany in 1963. The last sentence in the paragraph is the clincher sentence. It sums up the main idea of the paragraph in different words. The sentences between the topic sentence and the clincher sentence all present specific details about the situation in West Berlin and some of the events that led to tensions between the East and the West during the Cold War.

It is useful to think of a paragraph as being like a hamburger. The topic sentence is the bun on top. The clincher sentence is the bun at the bottom. The meat of the paragraph and all its dressings are the supporting details that appear in the middle.

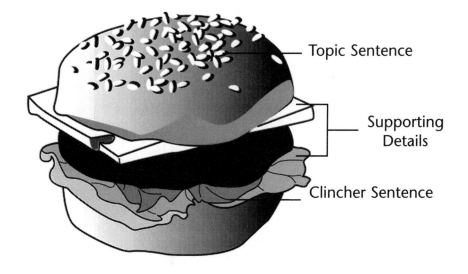

Topic Sentence

Supporting Details

Clincher Sentence

Follow these steps when writing a paragraph:

Writing a Paragraph, Step by Step

Step 1: Make a rough outline of the paragraph on scrap paper. Jot down the main idea that will be your topic sentence. Then, beneath the main idea, use dashes to introduce your supporting details. In a paragraph on a DBQ test, your supporting details will be information from the documents you have studied.

Kennedy's visit to West Berlin to show support & spread good will

—city divided after WWII into East and West

—cold war political tensions

—Soviet blockade and Berlin airlift

—Built Berlin wall, no freedom or escape for the people

—"Ich bin ein Berliner" speech showed support to West Berliners

This paragraph happens to contain a lot of supporting details. However, usually three or four supporting details will be enough.

Step 2: Look over your rough outline. Make sure that your supporting details are in a sensible order, such as time order or order of importance. If necessary, rearrange your details.

Step 3: Write the supporting detail sentences, following your outline. Try to vary the beginnings and the lengths of your sentences, and make sure that every sentence begins with a capital letter. If you wish to do so, quote directly from one or more of your source documents. Make sure to put any such quotations in quotation marks.

Step 4: Write a clincher sentence that restates the main idea of the paragraph in other words.

Step 5: Proofread the paragraph for errors. Reread it carefully. Make sure that you have

- indented the first line of the paragraph
- used complete sentences
- spelled each word correctly
- used a capital letter at the beginning of each sentence
- used a capital letter at the beginning of each proper noun or adjective
- used an end mark, such as a period, question mark, or exclamation mark, at the end of each sentence.

LESSON 3.1

Exercise A. Writing Good Sentences

Directions:

Rewrite the following sentences and passages, correcting the errors in them.

1. On april 1 1999 canada created a new territory the territory was called nunavut it was carved out of the eastern portion of the northwest territories.

_____

_____

_____

2. the word <u>Nunavut</u> means "our land" in inuktitut inuktitut is the language of the inuit people.

_____

_____

_____

3. the inuit lived in Canada. before the europeans came.

_____

_____

_____

4. The territory was established as part of the nunavut land claims agreement act the agreement was signed in 1993.

_____

_____

_____

5. the new territory has its own flag in the upper right hand corner of this flag is the north star. A traditional guide for navigation.

_____

_____

_____

_____

_____

_____

6. Two of the colors of the flag of nunavut are blue and gold these colors symbolize the riches of the sky sea and land the other colors are red and white these are the national colors of canada.

_____

_____

_____

_____

_____

_____

_____

Exercise B. Making a Rough Outline

Directions:

Use information from the photographs on pages 3 and 4 to make a rough outline for a paragraph about the working conditions in the cotton mills in North and South Carolina.

_____

_____

_____

_____

_____

_____

_____

_____

_____

_____

Exercise C. Writing a Paragraph

Directions:

On your own paper, write a paragraph based on the outline that you made for Exercise B. Make sure that your paragraph contains a topic sentence, several body sentences containing information from the photographs, and a clincher sentence.

LESSON 3.2: WRITING PARAGRAPHS FOR THE SOCIAL STUDIES

In Lesson 3.1, you learned how to write good sentences and you learned about proper paragraph form. In this lesson you're going to study one student's paragraph to learn how it is put together. Below is how one student answered the written response question from the Pretest:

header

title

Leon Walker
September 1

Child Labor

topic sentence

In the late 1800s and early 1900s many children under 16 worked instead of going to school, but eventually new laws were passed to change the situation. Three documents show the situation of child workers. For example, a graph from New Jersey in 1903 shows that 73 percent of child laborers worked in factories. Pictures from North and South Carolina show that children often worked in very basic and dirty conditions. Jane Addams wrote that some little girls were working fourteen hours a day in a candy factory. They were exhausted and could not stand the sight of candy. Many people thought that there should be changes to child labor laws because of the long hours and poor working conditions. For example, an editorial from Good Housekeeping magazine shows how Georgia changed its laws to ones that were "as good as any of which we have knowledge." In 1938, the government passed the Fair Labor Standards Act. This Act made laws about the age, hours, wages, and conditions for child laborers. A poster created to support the Act said that children under 16 belonged in school and that education was their full-time job. During the industrial revolution, children were working hard in difficult situations, and people did not think that this was right, so many states and the U.S. government changed the laws to make the situation better for children.

supporting detail #1

supporting detail #2

supporting detail #3

supporting detail #4

supporting detail #5

supporting detail #6

clincher

Exercise A. Analyzing a Paragraph

Directions:

Review the documents on pages 3–9. Then reread the sample paragraph by Leon Walker on page 89. Finally, answer the following questions about Leon's paragraph.

1. What is the question for which Leon's paragraph is the answer? (See page 10.)

_____

_____

_____

2. What is the topic sentence in Leon's paragraph? Where does the topic sentence appear?

_____

_____

_____

3. What documents did Leon use to support the idea that working conditions were not very good for children?

_____

_____

_____

4. What documents did Leon use to tell about changes that were made in child labor laws?

_____

_____

5. Did Leon quote from any of the documents? Where did he use quotes?

_____

_____

_____

6. What are the two parts of the question that Leon answered? Does his paragraph answer both parts of the question? How does Leon do that?

_____

_____

_____

_____

_____

_____

7. Did Leon use all of the source documents from pages 3–9 in his paragraph? Explain.

_____

_____

_____

LESSON 3.2

Exercise B. Outlining a Paragraph

Directions:

Write a rough outline of Leon's paragraph below.

_____

_____

_____

_____

_____

_____

_____

Exercise C. Planning a Paragraph

Directions:

Choose a topic from current events reported in the newspaper. Find two or three newspaper articles or graphics about the topic. If you wish, you can use one Internet source as well. Study your sources, then make a complete plan for a paragraph about the topic. Fill in the following form to show what you plan to do in your paragraph:

Topic of Paragraph:

_____

_____

Topic Sentence:

_____

_____

Supporting Detail 1:

_____

_____

Supporting Detail 2:

_____

_____

Supporting Detail 3:

_____

_____

Clincher Sentence:

_____

_____

Exercise D. Writing a Paragraph

Directions:

On your own paper, write a draft of the paragraph that you planned in Exercise C. Make sure that your paragraph has a topic sentence, supporting details, and a clincher sentence.

Exercise E. Proofreading a Paragraph

Directions:

Reread your draft paragraph, proofreading it for errors. Follow the checklist for proofreading given below.

Proofreading Symbols

Symbol and Example	Meaning of Symbol
∧ bicycle built for two	Insert (add) something that is missing.
Paris in the the spring	Delete (cut) these letters or words.
extreme estreme skiing	Replace this letter or word.
the glass delicate slippers	Transpose (switch) the order.
give to the needy gifts	Move this word to where the arrow points.
chair person	Close up this space.
truely	Delete this letter and close up the space.
≡ five portuguese sailors	Capitalize this letter.
/ a lantern and a Sleeping bag	Lowercase this letter.
waves. "Help me!" she cried.	Begin a new paragraph
⊙ All's well that ends well	Put a period here.
∧ parrots macaws, and toucans	Put a comma here.
children's toys	Put an apostrophe here.
There are three good reasons	Put a colon here.
# the grand opening	Put a space here.

POSTTEST

This unit contains a Posttest.

You will have an hour and a half to complete it.

POSTTEST: DOCUMENT-BASED QUESTION

Historical Background:

In 1835, Texas was still part of Mexico. On March 2, 1836, American settlers living in Mexican Texas rebelled against the Mexican government. They declared Texas an independent republic. Mexican President Antonio Lopez de Santa Anna led his army into Texas to put down the rebellion. His troops were defeated at the battle of San Jacinto in 1836, and Santa Anna was captured.

Texas was an independent republic for nine years even though the Mexican government still considered Texas to be Mexican territory. The American government wanted Texas to join the United States in 1845. Mexico was against having Texas join the United States, and many U.S. citizens were too. Some Americans were afraid that Texas would join the U.S. as a slave state. Mexico threatened war if the U.S. made Texas a state. Consequently, the U.S. stationed troops in Texas.

In 1846, talks on the Texas question between the U.S. and Mexico broke down, and troops on both sides were put on alert. Tensions increased between the two sides. In April of 1846, General Mariano Arista crossed the disputed border of the Rio Grande river with his army and fighting began. President James K. Polk heard about the fighting and ordered a meeting with Congress. Congress declared war against Mexico on May 13, 1846.

The U.S.-Mexican War was fought from 1846 to 1848. In September of 1847, the U.S. Army under General Winfield Scott occupied Mexico City.

Peace was negotiated in the spring of 1848. Mexico agreed to set the border with the U.S. at the Rio Grande river and agreed to let the U.S. make Texas a state. Mexico also gave up land in New Mexico and California but kept its territory in Baja California.

Task:

Write a paragraph that answers the following question:

Today Mexico and the United States are peaceful neighbors. How was the relationship different in the years from 1836 to 1848?

Before writing your paragraph, study the documents that follow and answer the scaffolding questions about them.

Part A: Scaffolding Questions

Directions:

Answer the questions that follow the documents. Use information from the documents and your own knowledge. Your answers will help you to write the paragraph in Part B.

The Mexican government ... invited and induced the Anglo-American population of Texas to colonize its wilderness under the pledged faith[1] of a written constitution, that they should continue to enjoy that constitutional liberty and republican government to which they had been habituated[2] in the land of their birth, the United States of America. ...

It has failed and refused to secure, on a firm basis, the right of trial by jury, that palladium[3] of civil liberty, and only safe guarantee for the life, liberty, and property of the citizen. ...

It has demanded the surrender of a number of our citizens, and ordered military detachments to seize and carry them into the Interior for trial, in contempt of the civil authorities, and in defiance of the laws and the constitution. ...

It has demanded us to deliver up our arms. ...

It has invaded our country both by sea and by land, with intent to lay waste our territory, and drive us from our homes.

[1]pledged faith. promise
[2]habituated. accustomed
[3]palladium. protector

Excerpt from the Texas Declaration of Independence (March 2, 1836)

1. Why did Americans colonize territory in Mexican Texas?

_____

_____

2. What rights did the Mexican government deny the Texans?

_____

_____

3. What, according to the Texans, did Mexico do to "a number of [its] citizens"?

_____

_____

> *The victory of San Jacinto was one of no ordinary character, for it struck the fetters[1] forever off the hands of Texas, deciding at once a contest between an empire numbering eight million inhabitants and one of its small provinces[2] containing a handful of men. The first result of the battle was to drive back the standard[3] of Mexico, compelling it to retire beyond the Rio Grande, never to return except in predatory and transient incursions.[4] This victory opened the way for American progress toward the South. Such was the immediate outcome of the battle, while the annexation[5] of Texas and the result of the Mexican war gave us additional territory equal… to one-third of the then United States.*
>
> [1]**fetters.** chains
> [2]**provinces.** regions
> [3]**standard.** flag or other symbol of a military unit or state
> [4]**predatory and transient incursions.** short raids to rob and murder
> [5]**annexation.** addition of territory

Excerpt from *The Century*, August, 1884

4. What were two results of the battle of San Jacinto?

_____

_____

5. What kind of relations does this article suggest the U.S. had with Mexico at the time of the battle of San Jacinto (in 1836)?

_____

_____

ANTI-TEXAS MEETING

AT FANEUIL HALL!

Friends of Freedom!

A proposition has been made, and will soon come up for consideration in the United States Senate, to annex Texas to the Union. This territory has been wrested from Mexico by violence and fraud. Such is the character of the leaders in this enterprise that the country has been aptly termed "that valley of rascals." It is large enough to make *nine* or *ten* States as large as Massachusetts. It was, under Mexico, a free territory. The freebooters have made it a slave territory. The design is to annex it, with its load of infamy and oppression, to the Union. The immediate result may be a war with Mexico—the ultimate result *will be* some 18 or 20 more slaveholders in the Senate of the United States, a still larger number in the House of Representatives, and the balance of power in the hands of the South!

All opposed to this scheme, of whatever sect or party, are invited to attend the meeting at the Old Cradle of Liberty, to-morrow, (Thursday Jan. 25,)at 10 o'clock, A. M., at which time addresses are expected from several able speakers.

Bostonians! Friends of Freedom!! Let your voices be heard in loud remonstrance against this scheme, fraught with such ruin to yourselves and such infamy to your country.

January 24, 1838.

Excerpt from a poster announcing meeting against the annexation of Texas to the U.S.

6. According to the creators of this poster, what was Texas like under Mexican rule?

_____

_____

7. What two warnings does the poster give against making Texas part of the United States?

_____

_____

> *To the Senate and House of Representatives:*
>
> *The existing state of the relations between the United States and Mexico renders it proper that I should bring the subject to the consideration of Congress....*
>
> *Mexico has passed the boundary of the United States, has invaded our territory and shed American blood upon the American soil. She has proclaimed that hostilities[1] have commenced,[2] and that the two nations are now at war....*
>
> [1]**hostilities.** fighting
> [2]**commenced.** begun

War Message from President James K. Polk to Congress on May 11, 1846

8. What is the purpose of this statement?

_____

_____

_____

9. What does this statement tell you about the relationship between the U.S. and Mexico in 1846?

_____

_____

_____

_____

Currier & Ives print of General Winfield Scott, known as "Old Fuss and Feathers," reviewing troops on horseback in 1846. Scott was responsible for capturing Mexico City in September, 1847. After the capture of Mexico's capital, the fighting between the U.S. and Mexico began to die down, and peace was declared in 1848.

10. What does this illustration show?

_____

_____

11. What does this picture suggest about General Scott?

_____

_____

_____

12. How did General Scott's actions affect the relationship between Mexico and the U.S.?

_____

_____

_____

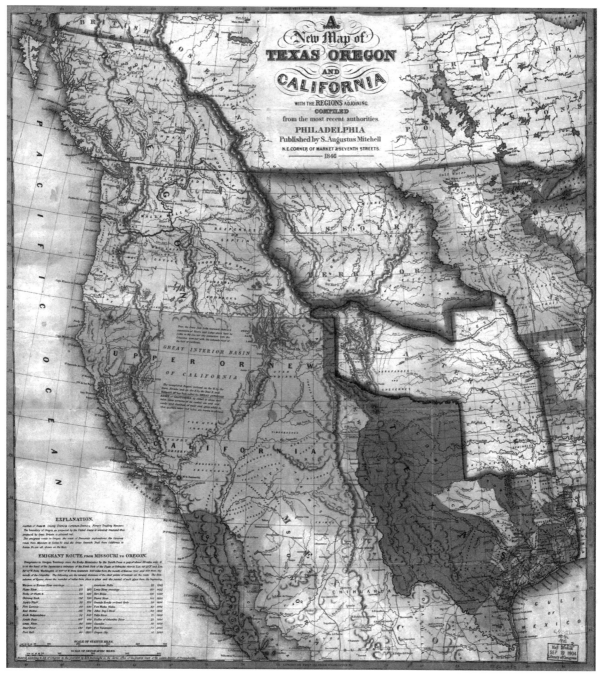

A map of Texas, Oregon, and California created in 1846

13. As a result of the war with Mexico, the U.S. won the territories of Texas, New Mexico, and California. What does this map tell you about the size of the new territory?

_____

_____

Part B: Paragraph Response

Directions:

Use your answers from Part A to write a paragraph. Answer this question: Today Mexico and the United States are peaceful neighbors. How was the relationship different in the years from 1836 to 1848? In your paragraph, use examples from the documents to support your ideas.

In your paragraph, remember to include
- a topic sentence, or opening sentence, that tells what your paragraph will be about;
- supporting sentences that use examples from the documents to support the idea in your topic sentence;
- a clincher sentence, or ending sentence, that ends your paragraph and finishes your idea.

STOP

Acknowledgments (cont. from page ii)

Courtesy The Hearst Corporation, *Good Housekeeping,* p. 7. Historical Labor Statistics Project, University of California, Riverside, pp. 5, 36. Historical Statistics of the United States: Colonial Times to 1970, U.S. Census Bureau, p. 43. Library of Congress: American Memory, African-American Pamphlet Collection, p. 79. Library of Congress: American Memory, Broadsides and Printed Ephemera Collection, pp. 30, 31, 33, 77, 99. Library of Congress: American Memory, First Person Narratives of California's Early Years, p. 55. Library of Congress: American Memory, Nineteenth Century Periodicals, pp. 61, 66, 98. Library of Congress: American Memory, Prosperity and Thrift: The Coolidge Era and the Consumer Economy, 1921–1929, p. 76. Library of Congress: American Memory, Work Projects Administration Poster Collection, pp. 28, 32. Library of Congress, Geography and Map Division, pp. 41, 103. Library of Congress, Prints and Photographs Division, p. 63, LC-USZ62-2578 DLC p. 19, LC-USZ62-52430, p. 56, LC-USZC2-2800, p. 101. Library of Congress, Prints and Photographs Division, FSA/OWI Photograph Collection, LC-USF 33-011402-M4, p. 44. Library of Congress, Prints and Photographs Division, George Grantham Bain Collection, LC-USZ62-99675, p. 17. National Archives, Center for Legislative Archives, p. 20. National Archives, Civilian Records, p. 53. National Archives, Still Picture Branch, p. 34. National Archives, Still Picture Branch, Department of Commerce and Labor, Children's Branch, pp. 3, 4, 14. National Archives, Still Picture Branch, Office of Government Reports, pp. 6, 25. National Archives, Still Picture Branch, U.S. Information Agency, pp. 22, 23. National Archives, Still Picture Branch, Work Projects Administration, p. 21. National Center for Education Statistics, p. 37. The Making of America Digital Collection, Cornell University Library, pp. 64, 65, 67. United States Environmental Protection Agency, p. 38. U.S. Census Bureau, pp. 40, 42. The authors and editors have made every effort to trace the ownership of all copyrighted pieces found in this book and to make full acknowledgment for their use.

A C K N O W L E D G M E N T S

INDEX

A

account. See *eyewitness account.*
act, 9, 69
actions, in photographs and illustrations, 15
Addams, Jane, 8, 46
adult education, 28
advertisement, 25–32, 33
African-American, civil rights 22–24, 78–80; leaders, 54
Alaskan gold fields, 41
allies, 75, 83
amendment, 73, 78
analysis, 12, 16
analyzing test questions, 11–12
Arbor Day, 77
Arista, Mariano, 96
Arizona, 77
Asian/Pacific languages, 42
audience, for ad or poster, 27

B

Baja California, 96
bar graph, 36, 37, 40, 43
Battle of Gettysburg, 48
Battle of San Jacinto, 96, 98
Bell, Dr. Alexander Graham, 51–52
Berlin, 83, 84, 85; airlift, 83, 85; wall, 83, 85
bias, See *perspective.*
bill, 69, 71
birth certificate, 69
Booth, Edmund, 55
border, 96
Breckinridge, John C., 63
Brodie, Alexander O., 77

C

California, 55; new map of, 103. See also *Gold Rush.*
Canada, 31, 61, 86–87
Canadian gold fields, 41
capitalization, 81–82, 85
caption, 12, 15, 47, 59
Charter of the United Nations, 75
Chicago fire, 66–68
Chief Joseph, 49–50
child labor, 2–10; laws, 7, 71
civilian labor force, 40
civil rights, early struggle for, 78–80; march on Washington, D.C., 22–24
clincher sentence, 10, 83, 84, 85, 104
Cold War, 83, 84, 85
comparison, 12
compass rose, 37

Congress, 96, 100
Connecticut, 63
Constitution, 69, 73, 78
contrast, 12
Coolidge, Calvin, 76
copy, 26
cotton mills, 3–4, 14, 88
covered wagons, 34
Cuzco, 39

D

DBQ. See *document-based question.*
DBQ paragraph, 89–94
decision, 69
declaration, 69
deed, 69
de Santa Anna, Antonio Lopez, 96
description, 12
detail, in informational graphic, 37; in letter or eyewitness account, 47; in map, 37; in newspaper or magazine article, 59. See also *supporting detail.*
diary, 46
document, 11
document-based question, defined, 11; examples of, 2–10, 22–24, 33–35, 43–45, 55–57, 66–68, 78–80, 96–104
Douglass, Frederick, 54

E

education, 65
Emperor Pachacuti, 39
Emperor Topa, 39
end marks, 81, 85
excerpt, 59
Executive Order, 76
eyewitness account, 46–54; contrasted with newspaper article, 58

F

fact, versus opinion, 46; in newspaper articles, 58
Fair Labor Standards Act, 6, 9, 25, 71
Federal Art Project, 28, 32
federal workers, 76
Fifteenth Amendment, 73
Fourth of July, 54
fragment, 82

G

Georgia, 7, 58
Germany, 53, 83, 84, 85
Gold Rush, 55–57

government documents, 69–77
governor, 77
graphic, 36
graphic organizer, for paragraphs, 84
Great Britain, 53, 83
Great Depression, 43–45

H

heading, in advertisement or poster, 26; of informational graphic, 37; in magazine article, 59
headlines, 59
Hine, Lewis W., 3, 4, 14, 21
House of Representatives, 100
Hull-House, 8, 46

I

Illinois Safety Division, 32
illustration, 14–21, 101
immigrants, 81–82
inaugural ceremony, 19
Inca, 39
Incan Empire, 39
indention, 85
indigenous peoples, 39, 49, 86–87
Indo-European languages, 42
inference, 16, 59
informational graphics, 36–42
interpretation, 12
Inuit, 86
Inuktitut, 86

J

Jackson, William Henry, 56
jobs, 22, 32, 43, 76
journalist, 58
judgment, 69

K

Keller, Helen, 51–52
Kennedy, John F., 83, 84, 85
key, 37
key word, 12
Klondike, 41

L

label, of informational graphic, 37
language change, 58
law, 69
Lee, Russell, 44
legend, 37
legislative record, 69
letter, 46–54, 51–52, 55; business, 46; to the editor, 46
Lincoln, Abraham, 19, 63
Lincoln Hall, 49
longshoremen, 21

INDEX

M

machines, 3, 4, 14–16
Machu Picchu, 39
magazine article, 7, 58–65, 66, 67, 98
main idea, of letter or eyewitness account, 47; of government document, 72; of newspaper or magazine article, 58, 59; of topic sentence, as in paragraph, 12
map, 36–37, 41, 103
marriage certificate, 69
marriage license, 69
Massachusetts, 79
Mexican, army, 96; cession of territory, 53, 96, 103; colonization laws, 97; Texas, 96
Mexico, 17, 21, 53
Mexico City, 17, 96, 101
minorities, 81–82
minutes, 69
Missouri Pacific Railroad, 33

N

Native Americans, 49
navigation, 87
Nazis, defeat of, 83
Nebraska, 34
new inventions, 64
New Jersey Bureau of Statistics of Labor and Industries, 5, 36
newspaper article, 58–65
New York City, 44
New York-Cuba Mail Steamship Line, 21
Nez Perce, 49
Nineteenth Amendment, 73
North Atlantic Treaty, 75
North Carolina, 3, 14, 88
north star, 87
Northwest, 61
Northwest Territories, 86
notetaking, 12, 18, 29, 39–40, 49–50, 61–62, 74
Nunavut, 86–87; flag of, 87; Land Claims Agreement Act, 86

O

objects, in photographs and illustrations, 15
official government document, 69–77
opinion, versus fact, 46
Oregon, new map of, 103

P

Page, Walter, 53
paragraph, 81–88; defined, 83; graphic organizer for, 84; outlining, 92; parts of, 84; planning, 92; proofreading, 94; step-by-step instructions for, 85
pardon, 69

peace, 49, 96, 101
perspective, 47
photograph, 3, 4, 14–21, 22–24, 34, 44, 56
pie chart, 5, 36, 38, 42
Polk, James K., 96, 100
poor, 81–82
poster, 6, 25–32, 99
Preamble, 75
presidential election, 63
primary source, 11
print, 101
proceedings, 69
proclamation, 70, 77
proofreading, 85, 94
proper adjective, 82
proper noun, 82
purpose, of ad or poster, 27; of letter or eyewitness account, 47; of government document, 71

Q

quotation marks, 82

R

railroads, 39
regulation, 70
reporter's questions, 12, 26, 59
Revolutionary War, 47
Rio Grande, 96, 98
Rochester, NY, 54
Roosevelt, Eleanor, 81–82
Roosevelt, Franklin D., 81–82
rough outline, 85, 88, 92
run-on, 82

S

San Francisco earthquake, 20
safety, 32
scaffolding question, 3–9, 11, 97–103
scale, 37
schools, 37
Scott, Winfield, 96, 101–102
secondary source, 11
Secretary of Labor, 9, 71
segregation, 22
Senate, 100
sentences, 81–82, 86–87
sequence, 37
setting, of letter or eyewitness account, 47; of newspaper or magazine article, 59
slavery, 78, 80
slogan, 26
source. See *primary source* and *secondary source.*
South Carolina, 4, 63, 88
Southern Confederacy, 63
Soviet, blockade of Berlin, 83, 85
speaker, in eyewitness account, 47
speech, 49, 54, 70, 83, 85, 100

spelling, 85
spinner, 4
statute, 70
subject, of a photograph, 15; of a sentence, 81
Sullivan, Annie M., 51–52
Sumner, Charles, 79
support, 12
supporting detail, 11; in a government document, 72; in a paragraph, 84, 85, 89–91, 93
surroundings, in photographs and illustrations, 15
Swing, David, 66

T

tax form, 70
teachers, 37, 51–52
Texas, annexation of, 96, 99; Declaration of Independence, 97; new map of, 103; Republic of, 96
Thirteenth Amendment, 78
timeline, 37, 39–40
title, 12; of informational graphic, 37; of newspaper or magazine article, 59; of photo or illustration, 15
topic sentence, 10, 11, 12, 84, 85, 89, 104
Tory, 47
trade, 21
treaty, 70, 71, 75
type, of government document, 71

U

unemployment, 40, 43–45
U.S. Department of Labor Children's Bureau, 6, 25
U.S.-German relations, 53
U.S.-Mexican relations, 53, 96–104
U.S.-Mexican War, 96–104

V

variables, in bar graphs, 37
verb, 81
von Eckhardt, Heinrich, 53
voting rights, 22, 73

W

Washington, D.C., 49
waste, 38
westward travel, 33–35
White House, 76
will, 70
Wilson, Woodrow, 53
women, equal rights of, 82
World War I, 53
World War II, 83, 85

Z

Zimmermann, Arthur, 53
Zimmermann telegram, 53

INDEX